Lessons From A Rainbow

Derek Stringer

British Library Cataloguing In Publication Data
A Record of this Publication is available
from the British Library

ISBN 978-1-84685-645-7

First Published 2007 by
Exposure Publishing,
an imprint of
Diggory Press Ltd
Three Rivers, Minions, Liskeard, Cornwall, PL14 5LE, UK
and of Diggory Press, Inc.,
Goodyear, Arizona, USA
WWW.DIGGORYPRESS.COM

Good News Broadcasting Association (UK)
Ranskill DN22 8NN England Email: info@gnba.net
Web site: www.gnba.net

Why 'Lessons From A Rainbow'?

The story of Noah and the Ark is one of the oldest and best-known stories in the world. Many different cultures have a story about a flood. When I was a child, we had a word for stories like this. We called them "whoppers." This is an amazing and incredible story. Let me illustrate.

A Skit . . .

Tom: *Well, it's another day at the office. Let's see what I need to do today.*

God: *Tom.*

Tom: [Picking up the telephone.] *Tom speaking how can I help you?*

God: *Tom.*

Tom: *Yes, who's there?*

God: *Tom, it's me* [echoing].

Tom: *Who is this?*

God: *Put down the phone, Tom. It's me . . . GOD* [echoing].

Tom: [Putting down the phone] *What is this?*

God: *I have a mission for you.*

Tom: *Is this some kind of joke?*

God: *This is no joke, Tom. I have decided to destroy the world.*

Tom: *Oh my God.*

God: *Yes, Tom. Listen carefully. There is an invisible, undetectable wave of subatomic particles travelling through space. It is headed toward your planet. It will reach the earth in one hundred years. When it hits, every living thing will die.*

Tom: *Are you sure you want to do that?*

God: *As much as it breaks my heart, yes. I cannot stand the evil any longer.*

Tom: *Should I warn everybody?*

God: *Yes, but it will not do any good. They will not listen. I've tried.*

Tom: *You said you had a mission for me?*

God: *Yes. I want you to build a space shuttle. After it is built, I will gather two of every living creature - male and female - to travel with you into space. When the wave of destruction has passed, you will return to earth. This is the only way to save my creation.*

Tom: *Whatever you say, Lord.*

God: *Here are the plans for the space shuttle. [Pause] You may want to take this down. It will take you almost one hundred years to complete the project. Are you ready?*

Tom: *Yes, Lord.*

God: *You shall make the space shuttle out of gopher fibres. You shall make the space shuttle with plenty of rooms. You shall cover it inside and out with pitch to protect against the subatomic wave. Are you getting this?*

Tom: *Yes, Lord. But could you do me one favour?*

God: *State your request.*

Tom: *Would you please clear this with my wife, because she is never going to believe me?*

How would you like to come home and tell your wife that story? It is an amazing and incredible story. It is also a very disturbing one. In our day and time, we have a tendency to focus on the sweet, furry animals coming two-by-two onto Noah's Ark. We like to talk about the animals and the rainbow. But we forget that as a result of the flood every living human being, with the exception of eight, died. What could Noah and the Ark possibly teach us? What does this story tell us about who God is and how He acts? We will get that information as we explore the story in this book.

Book Title? . . .

Let me explain the title of the book. The story of Noah and the Ark has to teach us that when God's holiness demands judgement, God's love delivers grace. Isn't that beautiful? A group of theologians from different faiths and religions gathered in London, England, to discuss religion. On one particular day they were considering the question: "What separates Christianity from all other religions?" That is a great question. Is there anything about Christianity that is different or distinguishes it from every other faith? Quite frankly, the theologians were stumped until C. S. Lewis walked into the room. C. S. Lewis had a simple answer when he heard the question: "What separates Christianity from all other religions?" C.S. Lewis said, "That's easy. It's grace."

After the flood waters had receded only eight people walked out on dry land. God came to Noah to make a "covenant" (Gen.9). God said, "I will never again destroy the earth with a flood." God signed His special contract of grace. Have you seen God's signature? God signed the sky. The rainbow is God's signature of grace.

Science explains the rainbow. As the waves of light pass through the prism created by the drops of water in the rain clouds, the light ray is separated into different bands of colour creating the display we see in the sky. All that is true but does not diminish the point that God makes as a lesson from the rainbow. The next time we look at a rainbow ask, "What kind of God do I know?" The story of Noah can help us answer correctly. That is important both for time and eternity.

Lessons From A Rainbow

Contents

Chapter 1   9
Why Such A Great Disaster?
Genesis 6:1-8

Chapter 2   23
Noah's Ark: A Picture Of Salvation
Genesis 6:9-22

Chapter 3   37
Hope For Those Who Feel Forgotten
Genesis 7-8

Chapter 4   51
Judgement First, Then Mercy
Genesis 9:1-17

Chapter 5   65
The Problem Of Racism
Genesis 9:18-10:32

Chapter 6   79
The Work Of Faith
Hebrews 11:7

Chapter 1
Why Such A Great Disaster?
Genesis 6:1-8

As we begin a book about Noah and the flood, I would like to focus your attention on a very crucial point: If this story is true, that is, if it really happened, and if there once was a great flood that covered the entire earth, then what the Bible is describing in Genesis 6 to 9 is the single greatest natural disaster in the history of the world. It is so great, vast and enormous, that no other event in earth's history comes close to it. It's Number One and there really is no Number Two.

A few days ago I went on the Internet using *Google* and just put in the words *Top Ten Natural Disasters.* Immediately it showed me a selection by David Crossley, Professor of Geophysics. He wrote: "Defining 'worst' is, of course, subjective, and leads to a choice over whether the number of deaths, or dollar property damage, is the statistic to use. Here is a representative collection of some of the 'big ones', organised in more or less inverse chronological order." He goes on to say, "The October 8, 2005 magnitude 7.6 earthquake in Pakistan was not especially large, but the more than 40,000 victims has raised it to the level of a major catastrophe. Without doubt, however, the most devastating loss of life in recent years was the much larger 9.3 Sumatra-Andaman earthquake (the third largest ever recorded) tsunami in late 2004 that is now estimated to have claimed 275,000 lives. Hurricane Katrina, however, was a major international story. The list contains several volcanoes. The most devastating earthquake in modern times was the famous 1976 Tangshan magnitude 8 event in China, whose toll varies between the official 255,000, and a possible 655,000." Then he adds, "Considerable evidence exists for a major global paleoclimate event that happened around 3000B.C. It appears to have affected sea-level changes, vegetation and much surface chemistry. There is speculation that this event is in fact the Biblical Flood of the Old Testament. Scientists naturally avoid equating 'natural' disasters with 'Acts of God', but in this case the time coincidence is very suggestive.

Other lists leave out Noah's Flood completely. But Genesis describes a vast flood that covered the entire earth. The event itself is so stupendous as to be mind-boggling."

Trying to think about a flood of that magnitude, one question keeps floating to the surface. Why would God do such a thing? The Bible states that the flood was a judgement on human sin. But what could the people of the pre-flood world have done that was so horrendous that it made God decide to hit the "Delete" button and wipe out all humanity with the exception of Noah and his family? What sort of sin brings on a judgement like the flood?

In order to answer that question, let's take a look at the words of Jesus in Matthew 24:37. This passage is part of a longer section called the Olivet Discourse, a private message given by Jesus to his disciples on the Mount of Olives two or three days before he was crucified. The subject is the return of our Lord to the earth at the end of the age. In order to help them understand that future event, Jesus draws a fascinating comparison with the days of Noah. He tells his disciples that the past is the key to the future. "As it was in the days of Noah, so it will be at the coming of the Son of Man. For in the days before the flood, people were eating and drinking, marrying and giving in marriage, up to the day Noah entered the ark; and they knew nothing about what would happen until the flood came and took them all away. That is how it will be at the coming of the Son of Man."

Study the days of Noah because what happened in those days will happen again at the end of this age. The spiritual conditions of the pre-flood world will be replicated in the days preceding the return of Christ to the earth. And what do we find when we examine the world of Noah's day? Write over it this phrase in large letters: BUSINESS AS USUAL. They were eating and drinking (nothing wrong with that), marrying and giving in marriage (nothing wrong with that). They were buying and selling and continuing in all the usual activities of human life. Children went to school each day, businessmen made deals, teachers taught, doctors dispensed healing, farmers tended their crops. They evidently paid no attention to "crazy Noah" and the big boat he was building in his back garden. Maybe he was regarded as a local whacko whose oddities were tolerated and made the butt of cocktail-hour humour. As he warned them of impending judgement, they paid him no mind whatsoever. But at last the day came when Noah entered the Ark. "The rains came down and the flood came up." I'm sure in that day the people started beating on the door but it was too late.

One translation of verse 39 says "they did not know." What a damning indictment. It was an age of enlightenment. But they did not know. It was an age of great progress. But they did not know. It was an age of music, fine arts and literature. But they did not know.

It was an age of military might. But they did not know. It was an age when mighty men roamed the earth. But they did not know. They knew so much but understood so little. They knew more and more about less and less until they knew everything about nothing and nothing about what really mattered. Professing themselves to be wise, they became fools. They had no time for God until it was too late. That is the world of Noah's day. They were wise fools who did not heed the warnings of the preacher of righteousness. Then the flood came and took them all away.

Genesis 6:1 to 8 offers the Bible's most detailed answer to the question, "Why did God send the flood?" Once sin entered the human bloodstream, it quickly spread until it dominated humanity. At first the serpent had to talk Eve into sin, then Adam sinned deliberately, then God couldn't talk Cain out of sin, then Lamech boasted about his brutality. But now, with the passing of a few generations, the entire world has become a cesspool of sin. Things have become so evil that God decides to start all over again.

What happened to bring on such a drastic judgement? Here are five phrases that help us grasp the reason God sent a world-wide flood.

Phrase 1: An Abuse of Marriage

Genesis 6:1, "When men began to increase in number on the earth and daughters were born to them, the sons of God saw that the daughters of men were beautiful, and they married any of them they chose."

Before we consider the controversial aspects of these verses, note the last two phrases. These marriages were made on the basis of nothing more than pure physical attraction. A man saw a woman and said, "I like her. She's beautiful. She's hot. I want her. She's mine." And he took her for himself. Forget about wisdom or training or education or ability or character. Don't worry about personality or family background. And certainly don't bother about godliness. Those things just get in the way. Marriage is now little more than the satisfaction of pure animal appetites. Man sees woman. Man wants woman. Man takes woman. The last phrase suggests a certain jumping of the boundaries God had established.

We know from Genesis 4 that Lamech felt free to take more than one wife. What would stop a man who lives only on the level of fleshly desire from having ten wives? Or 20? Or 30 (if he could afford them)? The real question regarding these verses involves the mysterious statement that the "The sons of God saw that the daughters of men." To whom do these phrases refer? In the history of biblical interpretation, there have been three main answers given to this hotly debated question.

First, some Bible students suggest that this refers to the intermarriage of believers with unbelievers. In this view the "sons of God" are the godly line of Seth and the "daughters of men" represent women from the ungodly line of Cain. The subsequent judgement comes because of the widespread spiritual contamination caused by such deliberate compromise. In favour of this view is the fact that the preceding chapters clearly show the development of two lines—the godly and the ungodly. And we know from many other warnings in the Bible that God forbids believers to deliberately marry unbelievers. This is always wrong. For a believer to knowingly marry someone who does not love the Lord is a compromise that leads to years of heartache. Sometimes our Christian young people get "moonstruck" with love and do some very foolish things. Nothing can be more foolish than a believer thinking that marriage will somehow convince an unbeliever to come to Christ. It rarely happens. In my experience, for every time it happens, there are a dozen times that the believer ends up in a divided marriage, with the children pulled in two different directions, with the unbelieving spouse unwilling to come to Christ, and the believer struggling to maintain his or her faith. This is not surprising since it's always easier to drag someone down than to lift another person up. I agree with the concern behind the first view but it does not seem to me to be the most natural reading of Genesis 6:1 and 2.

Second, some scholars suggest that the phrase "sons of God" is a technical term from the Ancient Near East that describes human rulers who were despots. We might call them "big-shots" today. These were the ancient tribal chieftains who were bullies and braggarts. The "daughters of men" refers to the multiple wives and concubines who made up the earliest harems. Again, this is a plausible view but it depends on evidence from outside the Bible.

Third, the oldest interpretation, suggests that the "sons of God" refers to angels who rebelled against God (we would call them demons), inhabited human bodies, married human women, and gave birth to the "nephilim" of verse 4 who roamed the earth as ancient tyrants and bullies. On its surface, the view seems strange and even bizarre but it is, in my judgement, what this passage is teaching. For one thing, the term "sons of God" in the Old Testament in all its other occurrences always refers only to angels. And this interpretation accords very well with Genesis 3:15, which emphasises Satan's long "war" against the "seed of the woman" that will eventually produce the Messiah. What better way to destroy the coming Messiah than to utterly corrupt the human race through the introduction of demonism? And this truly is the oldest interpretation. This is how the Jewish scholars who translated the Old Testament into Greek (the Septuagint) understood the text approximately two centuries before the birth of Christ.

This interpretation also helps us understand two cryptic passages in the New Testament: 2 Peter 2:4, "If God did not spare angels when they sinned, but sent them to hell, putting them into gloomy dungeons to be held for judgement; if he did not spare the ancient world when he brought the flood on its ungodly people, but protected Noah, a preacher of righteousness, and seven others." Jude 6, "The angels who did not keep their positions of authority but abandoned their own home – these he has kept in darkness, bound with everlasting chains for judgement on the great Day." Both passages describe a very drastic judgement upon certain angels who not only sinned but "abandoned their own home."

Note that in Peter, the angels are mentioned first, then comes Noah and the flood. In Jude the event is connected with the story of Sodom and Gomorrah.

Genesis 19 tells us that the men of Sodom and Gomorrah were ready to rape the two angelic visitors who appeared in human form. Put it all together and it looks like this: In the days before the flood, certain angels rebelled against God and entered human bodies in a form of demon-possession, taking for themselves human wives. The resulting cohabitation produced a form of evil offspring called the nephilim who roamed the earth as giants, tyrants, and workers of enormous evil. For this hideous sin, the angels were sent to the pit of deep darkness and the existing civilisation was wiped out in the great flood.

In the Gospels we learn that demons crave human bodies to inhabit.

When the "legion" of demons was cast out of the Gadarene demoniac, they begged to be allowed to enter a herd of pigs. Since we know such things are possible, it should not surprise us that the total rejection of God led to bizarre sexual sin and an outbreak of evil unprecedented in world history.

One final note. I lean to this view because the context seems to demand some sort of extraordinary sin that would cause God to wipe out an entire civilisation and start all over again. The hubris of those days was so great that men and women thought nothing of breaching the God-ordained boundaries on human conduct in the most evil way possible. Having said that, I also agree that this is a very difficult passage to interpret. We don't have enough in the text to be certain about the meaning. This is one of those places where we wish Moses had added a few footnotes.

Even though my interpretation is a fairly common interpretation, many notable interpreters take other views and they may well be correct. This is not an issue on the level of the Deity of Christ. No one can say with total certainty what the text means in Genesis 6:1 and 2. I simply have shared why I follow the view that I have. The first phrase to sum up those times is: *An Abuse Of Marriage.*

Phrase 2: An End to God's Patience.

"Then the Lord said, "My Spirit will not *contend* with man for ever, for he is mortal; his days will be a hundred and twenty years." In light of the bizarre morality of the pre-flood world, it is not surprising that God's patience finally wore thin. The word translated *"contend"* may also mean *"protect."* In that sense, this verse is both a warning and a promise of grace extended for a short period of time. I take it that the 120 years refers not to man's new life span, but to the years remaining before the flood. Up until now, God's Spirit has protected mankind from self-destruction, but at some point that protection will be removed and man will then be left to his own devices.

Write over this verse "Romans 1" because the message is the same. When men rebel against God, sooner of later he "gives them up" to face the consequences of their own sinful choices. God will not protect us from ourselves forever. Sooner or later, the bell tolls, judgement day arrives, and we have to face the music. In this case, it meant that in 120 years, the flood would come and take them all away. Until then, God's grace was extended by giving men a further period in which to repent.

Note that the story of the flood is used in precisely the same way in 2 Peter 3:1-9. There we learn that the seeming delay in God's judgement is not because he "winks" at sin but because he postpones judgement to give us more time to repent. But God's patience will not last forever. Let those who walk in sin be warned. If you think God doesn't see you or he doesn't care or perhaps that he doesn't even exist, you will one day be surprised by the sudden judgement of God. When hell opens to swallow you, it will be too late to cry out for mercy. To borrow a phrase from Langston Hughes,
"God gave Noah the rainbow sign
Said, 'No more water, the fire next time.'"

Phrase 3: An Abundance of Charismatic, Corrupt Leaders.

"The Nephilim were on the earth in those days—and also afterwards—when the sons of God went to the daughters of men and had children by them. They were the heroes of old, men of renown." Everyone agrees that verse 4 is difficult to interpret. The word "nephilim" is simply a transliteration of a Hebrew word that means something like "the fallen ones." It is sometimes translated "giants" and may in fact refer to a race of ancient men and women who were ten to 12 feet tall. I have mentally jotted beside this verse "Tower of Babel" because

these "nephilim" were a race of ancient leaders who in their arrogance ignored God, built vast empires, acted as despots and tyrants, and embodied the worst traits of humanism—living as if God did not exist. They would agree with the man who said,
"I am the master of my fate, the captain of my soul."

No doubt they were highly gifted individuals who could be charming when they needed to be but underneath were ravenous wolves, filled with corruption, violence, hatred and all manner of evil. Such men filled the earth in the days before the flood. Verse 4 seems to intimate that they were the offspring of the ungodly union of the "sons of God" and the "daughters of men."

Phrase 4: A Headlong Rush into Evil.

"The Lord saw how great man's wickedness on the earth had become, and that every inclination of the thoughts of his heart was only evil all the time" (v.5). Nowhere else in the Bible will you find such a clear description of the doctrine of Total Depravity. Here is mankind as God sees it. This is the human race wholly apart from God's grace.

In Genesis 1 we are repeatedly told that "God saw" what he had made and it was "good" and "very good." By Genesis 6 when God looks on the earth, he sees his creation turned into a foul cesspool of evil. If you want to know what sin is like, study this verse: First: Sin is internal. It is a matter of the heart first and foremost. "The thoughts of his heart." Second: Sin is pervasive. It touches every part of our existence. "Every inclination of the thoughts of his heart." Third: Sin is continual. It consumes man and controls him. "Every inclination of the thoughts of his heart was only evil all the time."

This is what you are apart from God's grace. Any "good" you may do is stained with the dirt of your own sinful inclinations. You have never done a truly good deed in and of yourself and you never will. All that we do is tainted with self-interest. Even

17

our good deeds are but "filthy rags" in the sight of Almighty God says Isaiah 64:6. Your heart is so wicked that you don't even know the half of your own sin. In the words of Anselm of Canterbury, *you have not yet considered how sinful you are.*

Do not read Genesis 6:5 and say, "Those people must have been terrible." Read it and then look in the mirror. There is no difference. That's the whole point of Romans 3:23. No difference between them and us. No difference between then and now. No difference between the savage in the jungle and the corporate executive who is under indictment. Take away his Masters in Business studies, his fine cut suit, his shiny new car, and underneath beats the heart of a sinner. All the thoughts of his heart are evil continually.

Phrase 5: A Shocking Judgement from Heaven.

"The Lord was grieved that he had made man on the earth, and his heart was filled with pain. So the Lord said, "I will wipe mankind, whom I have created, from the face of the earth— men and animals, and creatures that move along the ground, and birds of the air—for I am grieved that I have made them." Think about these phrases carefully: "The Lord was grieved" and "His heart was filled with pain." God's grief is a sign of his great love. The Lord is no robot. He is not some unfeeling God in heaven who sets the world in motion and then watches in benign disinterest while men and women destroy themselves. His heart breaks over the sin that covers the earth. He weeps over broken homes, broken promises, suffering children, and the wreckage of human sin that covers planet earth and turns it into a massive junkyard of pain, sadness, shame and guilt. So now God decides to "uncreate" the earth. Think of what this means. Whole cities destroyed. Homes washed away. Roads covered. Buildings inundated. Whole villages flooded. Men, women and children vanishing beneath the waves. The whole earth under the waters of judgement. Nothing like it had happened before and nothing like it has happened since. It was a catastrophic judgement that enveloped the entire globe and washed away every vestige of human civilisation.

Only one man and his family are spared. "But Noah found *favour* in the eyes of the Lord." The word translated "favour" actually means "grace." Noah found "grace" in the eyes of the Lord. Because this is the first mention of "grace" in the Bible, it is hugely significant. The word means "undeserved favour." It describes the blessing God gives to those who don't deserve it. It is the "contrary-to-merit" favour of God. Do not read this verse and think, "Noah was a really good man, a righteous man, and because he obeyed God, he earned God's grace." That's impossible. It doesn't happen that way. Noah didn't "earn" anything. Grace was given to him the same way it is given to people today. Either grace is a gift or it isn't grace. Instead of saying, "Noah found grace," we should say instead, "Grace found Noah." That would be more appropriate. Grace found him and saved him and his whole family.

Let us learn two important truths from this verse.

(1) Grace is available in the darkest hours.

Even though the world was rushing headlong into judgement, Noah found grace. There is never a pit so deep that the love of God is not deeper still. Do not say, "I am too bad a sinner to ever be saved." You don't know that. Don't say, "God could never forgive me." Yes, he can. And he will, if you will cry out to him. And don't say, "My husband is too far gone to ever be saved" or "I'm going to stop praying for that person because she is a hopeless case." You don't know that. While there is life, there is hope. Leave the final judgement in the hands of the Lord. Keep praying. And if you do not know the Lord, seek him while he may be found. Turn to him. Come to him. Trust in him. This is the day of grace. Though a thousand perish at your side, though your friends and family turn away, there is hope for you and plentiful grace if you will only come to Jesus.

(2) Grace is the only means of escape.

Was Noah somehow "better" than his contemporaries? No, he was a sinner just like them. But he found grace and was spared. He turned to the Lord and was delivered. Hebrews 11:7 tells us that "by faith" Noah saved himself and his family. What Noah did, you can do. By grace we can be delivered even in the darkest days and from the deepest pit of sin. I admit that grace is a hard concept for us to grasp. I define it as God doing for us what we could never do for ourselves. It is God coming to our rescue when we were trapped in sin.

Perhaps an illustration will help. Imagine a few years ago. It's a Wednesday and you are a coal miner in Pennsylvania. Today you are working 240 feet underground. By accident a drill pierces through the wall of an abandoned mine shaft nearby. Suddenly millions of gallons of water rush toward you. Quickly you and your eight buddies run for safety. It's clear you will never make it to the mine entrance. In desperation you clamber over the rocks, searching for an air pocket as the water rises around you. At length you find a tiny space with a little bit of air. There you and your friends huddle together. It is cold and dark. As the water continues to rise, you wonder how long you can survive. Slowly the truth hits you. You are 240 feet underground. There is no way out. You can do nothing to save yourself. You cannot swim to safety. You cannot dig your way to the surface. You are trapped in the darkness. If someone far above you does not come to your rescue, you will die where you are. That is exactly what happens. Far above you rescue workers drill an air hole, sending in hot air that keeps you warm and pushes back the rising water. Unknown to you, hundreds of people work together to dig first one rescue shaft and then another. Finally, they break through, the capsule is lowered, and you are lifted to safety. When you were trapped, they came for you. When you could do nothing, they rescued you. When your life was nearly gone, they dug through and found you. Someone far above came for you and you were saved.

This is the grace of God. When we were trapped in the darkness of sin, someone far above us came down from heaven to rescue us. He left the comforts of heaven to dig through the layers of sin and guilt to set us free. Jesus knew where we were. He came to us in our darkness and he shone the light of freedom upon us.

We were trapped by sin and living in the darkness. The waters of judgement were rising around us. There was nothing we could do to help ourselves. If someone from above does not come for us, we're going to die. Someone came. His name is Jesus. He dug down to where we were to set us free. This is the grace of God!

We have noted the words of Jesus in Matthew 24. As it was in the days of Noah, so shall it be when Jesus returns. If you want to know what the future looks like, go back to the past. The days of Noah are the key to understanding the days to come.

What are the marks of the "days of Noah?" Here is my answer: The world completely unprepared for the coming judgement. Widespread moral perversion and the breakdown of the family. A sharp rise in Satanic activity and growing interest in the occult. Shocking failure of leaders we thought we could trust. Rejection of God's authority in the name of "freedom."

Believers standing alone against the world. As it was … So it shall be. As it was … So it is today.

I believe the "days of Noah" are upon us right now. And that's one reason I believe we should get ready for the return of the Lord Jesus Christ to the earth. I will not make any predictions about when He will come, I don't know and the Bible doesn't encourage me to speculate. I just say, be ready. Don't despair. If you know the Lord, stand strong. Speak the truth. Follow God's call and do not let the world's hostility intimidate you.

These are wonderful days to serve the Lord. Think of it. We may possibly be the generation privileged to see Christ return to the earth. If so, let's be busy about our business, spreading the good news, working for the Kingdom, being salt and light, serving the Lord with joy wherever we go. The best news for all of us is this - *grace* is available for those who want it. We are more sinful than we can ever believe and we are more loved than we could ever hope. We are more sinful than we think and God loves us more than we could imagine. If you want the grace of God, it's yours for the asking. Noah found grace in the eyes of the Lord. What about you?

Chapter 2
Noah's Ark: A Picture Of Salvation
Genesis 6:9-22

The story of Noah and the Ark is more popular than ever before. Even people who don't know the Bible and never come to church know about Noah, his big boat, and all those animals coming in two by two. Two giraffes. Two tigers. Two snails, inching forward slowly. Two rabbits. Two parakeets. Even two skunks! And most people know about the great flood and how the boat floated until the waters receded. Then the animals departed two by two by two. Finally the rainbow appeared and God gave his promise never again to send a great flood that would cover the entire earth. For those who doubt the popularity of this story, the evidence is everywhere. If you travel you will find Noah's Ark restaurants, Noah's Ark paintings, Noah's Ark music boxes, Noah's Ark T-shirts, Noah's Ark coffee mugs, Noah's Ark aprons, Noah's Ark earrings, and you'll even find on the Internet a recipe for Noah's Ark cakes. I was travelling across Wisconsin in the USA to speak at a Bible Conference and passed the largest water park in the United States located in the Wisconsin Dells which is called … Noah's Ark.

A few years ago a man named Robert Fulghum wrote an essay called *"All I really need to know I learned in kindergarten."* It was so popular that it spawned a number of spin-offs. I ran across one called, *"All I need to know I learned from Noah's Ark."*

1. Don't miss the boat.
2. Remember that we are all in the same boat.
3. Plan ahead. It wasn't raining when Noah built the Ark.

4. Stay fit. When you're 600 years old someone may ask you to do something really big.

5. Don't listen to critics, just get on with the job that needs to be done.

6. Build your future on high ground.

7. For safety's sake travel in pairs.

8. Speed isn't everything. The snails were on board with the cheetahs.

9. When you're stressed, float awhile.

10. Remember the Ark was built by amateurs, the Titanic by professionals.

11. No matter the storm, when you are with God there's always a rainbow waiting.

There are basically two ways to approach this very familiar story. The first is to focus on the controversial issues. Examples would be, What was the extent of the flood? Did it really cover the entire earth? How large was the ark? How did Noah get those animals into the ark? I would include in this category the very pressing question sometimes asked (usually by teenagers), How did Noah and his family keep the ark clean with all those animals inside? Those questions are useful and important and I hope to answer some of them as we continue in our study. But if we concentrate only on the controversial elements, we risk missing the larger message. Even though it is important to ask, "How did a flood cover the entire earth?" if we stop there we will miss the larger spiritual lessons the Lord intends for us to learn. It is worthwhile to enquire about the civilisation that perished, but the emphasis of the text is not on those who died, but on the one family that survived. That is where we need to focus our attention.

How did Noah and his family escape the terrible judgement of the flood? Our text reveals a number of important facts about Noah. If we consider these things, we will understand why he and his family survived the flood while the rest of the human race perished.

(1) Noah was a godly man.

"Noah was a righteous man, blameless among the people of his time, and he walked with God." This verse is the key to everything else. Noah was a righteous man. That means he believed in God and took his Word seriously. He was not a doubter or a sceptic. Like Abraham who would follow him many generations later, Noah believed God and his faith was counted as righteousness. His faith produced in him a lifestyle that was so categorically different from his contemporaries that he seemed blameless by comparison. Here was a man who walked with God and knew him intimately. Noah didn't merely know about God, he knew God and walked with him on a daily basis. This is a high honour since he and Enoch are the only two men in the Bible who are specifically said to have walked with God.

(2) Noah was a family man.

"Noah had three sons: Shem, Ham and Japheth." We know that Noah was married and that he and his wife had three sons, and each son was also married. Noah was the head of his household and the spiritual leader to his wife, his sons and his daughters-in-law."

(3) Noah was a unique man.

"Now the earth was *corrupt* in God's sight and was full of violence. God saw how corrupt the earth had become, for all the people on earth had corrupted their ways." These verses are placed here to stress the contrast between Noah and his generation. The word *"corrupt"* means *rotten* or *putrid* or *utterly foul*. It describes a world in the final stages of moral decomposition. Having rejected the Lord, the men and women of the world had sunk into a deep pit of violence, hatred, abuse, murder, dishonesty, and every ugly expression of the depravity of the human heart.

If we are honest with ourselves, we all think things that we would never dare to speak aloud (nor should we). The heart is wicked beyond belief. But in civilised society, many evil thoughts are left that way—as thoughts, never to be mentioned or spoken or written or acted upon. In the days before the flood, evil thoughts became evil words that ultimately led to acts of unspeakable atrocity, brutality, lust and perversion. The unthinkable became thinkable, then speak-able, then do-able. Finally the unspeakable was done openly and praise was given to those who did it openly. Romans 1 offers another picture of how this process works in society.

In the darkness of those days, one man stood out from the crowd. Noah was a bright shining light in the prevailing moral darkness. In an impure world, he was pure. In an unrighteous world, he was righteous. In a world that dismissed God, he walked with God.

He stood alone, believing God, building the ark, no doubt receiving much abuse, always confident that God could be trusted and that the flood would someday come to the world. If his friends called him "Crazy Noah," it did not bother him. Or if it bothered him, it did not stop him. He stood his ground, and God noticed.

(4) Noah was an obedient man.

"Noah did everything just as God commanded him." This verse comes immediately after God gives specific instructions for building the ark. Note the two things said in this verse: His obedience was complete: He did everything the Lord commanded. His obedience was absolute: He did everything just as the Lord commanded. Nothing halfway. There was no "Well, I think I'll build two decks instead of three" or "I think I'll use oak instead of gopher wood" or "Let's make it 350 cubits instead of 300 cubits long." And he didn't try to bargain with God about all those animals. Because he believed God when he said a flood was coming, he had no reason to question the design of the ark or the need to provide space for all the land animals. God said it and that settled it for Noah.

26

(5) Noah was a bold man.

This fact is implied in Genesis 6 and stated explicitly in 2 Peter 2:5, where Noah is called a "preacher of righteousness." He wasn't just a builder who knew how to construct an enormous boat. And he wasn't just a godly man who let his life speak for him. During the 120 years before the flood, Noah built the ark and he also preached righteousness to his own generation. I'm sure he warned them of judgement to come and invited them to join him in the ark. No one seemed to listen. Perhaps they were too busy to pay attention. After all, it seems as if no one had ever seen rain before. Certainly no one had ever seen a world-wide flood before. Why should they take Noah seriously? To his contemporaries he was like those people who preach on the street corners. It's always easier just to walk on by than to stop and listen.

Jesus made a direct comparison between the days of Noah and the days preceding his return to the earth. "As it was then, so it shall be again." The past is the key to the future. Go back to Noah's day and what do you find? Widespread unbelief and scepticism, a generation that had no time for the Almighty. Killing and violence on a daily basis. Human life was cheap. Sexual perversion was the rule of the day. Better yet, there were no rules. Men and women did as they pleased, and the result was a putrefying mass of evil so sickening that God decided to start all over again. On one level it was "business as usual," on another level it was "sin to the 12th power." That same combination of moral corruption and "business as usual" will be the order of the day when Jesus returns.

We do live in dangerous times. When I travel by car I listen to the radio a lot. Every hour the news is the same: Another killing in the Middle East, more threats of terrorism, more worries about bio-terrorism, and every other day a knife was being used on a teenager by a teenager. This is our world.

I often fly to speak at conferences. The security is getting even more demanding and intrusive. "Hold your arms out, please.

Take off your belt and your watch. Take your computer out of the case. Take your shoes off. Stand over here for closer inspection." By the time you get on the aeroplane, you can't help but look at the person next to you and wonder, "Could you be a terrorist?" "Are you hiding something?" This is our world. That's the sort of world Noah lived in before the flood. A world where violence was the rule of the day and no one could ever feel completely safe.

How did Noah manage to save himself and his family in such a negative environment? We are not left to wonder about the answer because it is spelled out for us in Hebrews 11:7. This is a powerful verse that I recommend that you read, then memorise and then teach to your own family. "By faith Noah, when warned about things not yet seen, in holy fear built an ark to save his family. By his faith he condemned the world and became heir of the righteousness that comes by faith."

We can break this verse down into four smaller statements that help us see what Noah did:

1) He believed what God said.
2) He built an ark to save his family.
3) He rejected the corruption of the world.
4) He and his family were delivered from destruction.

First, he believed. Then he built. In so doing he rejected the ways of the world. As a result, he saved his own family. While others mocked him to scorn, he and his boys laboured year after year, building that massive ship. Day after day they lugged huge pieces of gopher wood and put them carefully into place, one plank at a time. For decades no one knew what it was, but then it began to take shape. Eventually the ark was completed and the days drew near for the flood. Finally the rains began, the animals arrived, and Noah and his family entered the ark together. Then the door was shut, the floodwaters rose, and the ark lifted Noah and his family to safety. How did he do it? "By faith!"

Here is a message especially for all men. Fathers, listen up. Sons and brothers, pay attention. Husbands, think about this carefully. Single men, take notice. All men and all boys, heed this word. Noah was a righteous man who had great faith in God. His faith saved his entire family. But note this. Not one word is ever said about the faith of his wife or the faith of Shem, Ham or Japheth or their wives. But they must have had some faith. How do I know that? When Noah entered the ark, his wife went with him. Then Noah and Mrs. Noah entered the ark, their boys went with them. hen the boys entered the ark, their wives went with them. I don't know how much faith they had, but they had enough to follow the head of the family. And Noah had enough faith to inspire all of them to follow his example. That's the power of a godly leader. Noah's faith saved his entire family. He believed so deeply and obeyed so completely and walked so intimately with God that it was natural for his entire family to do what he did. They believed because he believed.

This is the power of a godly example. It is also the power of a godly husband and father. Men, God holds you accountable to set the pace for your entire family. Your wife looks to you for leadership. Your sons and daughters will be like you, for better or for worse. If you abdicate your responsibility, your wife will never be able to fully take your place. And if you live out your faith every day, it's natural and normal to expect your family to follow in your steps. For all of us, men and women alike, take heart from Noah's example. You can be godly in a very ungodly world. Let's stop complaining about the evil of the present day. As bad as things are, they were worse in Noah's day. Back then, there were only eight true believers in the whole world. There were probably more than that in your Church Service. We have far more spiritual advantages than Noah had. All we need is the courage to do what Noah did and to believe what God has said.

Noah was a godly man in an ungodly age, a bright light shining in the darkness. Because he had character and obeyed God when the world thought he was crazy, he ended up saving his own family. God bless him. And God bless all those who follow in his steps. Let there be no complaining about how hard things are. No excuses about how evil the world has become. Be a man of character. Be a woman of conviction. Stand on the Word of God and don't worry about what the world thinks. You'll save yourself, and by God's grace, you may save your family and many others besides.

Regarding the ark itself, there is a very specific design given. In verses 14 to 16 we have the design. Then, a very specific reason stated in verse 17, a very specific promise given in verse 18, and some very specific passengers are listed in verses 19 to 20, along with some very specific cargo in verse 21. Rather than go into great detail, I would simply point out that there is nothing mystical here at all. The text reads like a sober historical account of what actually happened. This is not a fantasy story made up simply to teach a moral. If we take Genesis 6 seriously, then we ought to conclude that God really did speak to Noah and told him to build the ark because a great flood was coming. And he really did tell him to bring the land animals into the ark in order to keep them alive until the flood was over.

Regarding the ark, I discovered a fascinating fact during my studies. The Hebrew word translated "ark" is used in only two places in the Old Testament. In both places it basically means "box" or "container." This is significant when you consider that the other occurrence of this particular Hebrew word comes in Exodus 2 where it refers to the basket in which the infant Moses was placed when his mother hid him in the bulrushes. It is not a coincidence that the "basket" of Exodus 2 is coated with "pitch," the same resinous material used in the ark Noah built. The major point here is that Noah's Ark was not like a motorboat or a yacht or a three-mast schooner. It was essentially an enormous container designed to keep Noah and his family and the animals afloat during the yearlong duration of the flood. It had no rudder because Noah didn't need to steer it. He just needed a boat that would float, which is exactly what God told him to build.

The ark itself was very large. No doubt about that. The Hebrew text of Genesis gives the measurements in "cubits," usually taken to equal 18 inches (although some authorities suggest a cubit could be as long as 45 inches). If we assume that a cubit was 18 inches, then the ark was 450 feet long, 45 feet high, and 75 feet wide. That means it was long and narrow and relatively low-slung, basically a floating barge. Various engineering studies have revealed that such a design ratio produces a vessel that is incredibly stable and almost impossible to capsize. The basic design is very similar to the massive super-tankers that ferry oil from the Middle East to around the world. Again using the 18-inch cubit, and allowing for three floors inside the ark, it contained at least 100,000 square feet of floor space. Total storage space was over 1.5 million cubic feet, roughly the capacity of 569 standard train carriages.

That brings us to a question: How many animals were on the ark? We can't answer that with certainty. We know that Noah was told to include a male and female of all the land animals. It is a mistake to jump to the conclusion that Noah had to bring two of each species on earth. Genesis 1 speaks of created "kinds" of animals, a category that clearly seems larger than the species level. Some authorities suggest that the total number of animals would have been no more than 2,000. Others suggest as many as 16,000. But suppose the number equals 50,000. Would the ark have been large enough to accommodate them?

The following quote comes from the Christian Answers web site: "Remember there are really only a few very large animals, such as the dinosaur or the elephant, and these could be represented by young ones. Assuming the average animal to be about the size of a sheep and using a railroad car for comparison, we note that the average double-deck stock car can accommodate 240 sheep. Thus, three trains hauling 69 cars each would have ample space to carry the 50,000 animals, filling only 37% of the ark. This would leave an additional 361 cars or enough to make five trains of 72 cars each to carry all of the food and baggage plus Noah's family of eight people. The Ark had plenty of space."

The question is thoroughly discussed on a number of creationist web sites, often in great detail. Suffice it to say that when the evidence is fairly considered, it is clear that the ark was easily large enough to deliver Noah and his family and the land animals safely through the flood. After considering the nature of the ark itself, it is important that we recall the spiritual lessons that arise from this story. Three obvious ones come to mind:

(1) God judges sin.

From the standpoint of those who perished, this is the central message. Though God is patient even in the face of outright rebellion and repeated blasphemy, his patience must eventually come to an end. God will not always strive with men.

Sin will be judged sooner or later. It is judged in this life through the suffering and pain that comes to those who presume to live life apart from God's holy commandments. And it is judged ultimately in eternity when the unrighteous are sentenced to everlasting punishment in hell. The flood stands as a stark reminder that no one gets away with sin forever. As Martin Luther King, Jr. put it, *"The arm of the universe is long, but it bends towards justice."*

(2) Even in judgement, God displays His grace.

Though the world perished, one man and his family were saved. God never leaves himself without a witness in the world. This truth saves us from despair when we see evil men rising to power and sin being praised openly. And it gives us great hope as we spread the gospel. Until the day the flood came, the door was open. Anyone could have entered.

(3) Judgement will come when Jesus returns to the earth.

This is the point Jesus makes in Matthew 24 when he compares the "days of Noah" to the days before his return to the earth. There was total unconcern with even the remote possibility of divine judgement. The men and women of Noah's day did not believe him, or perhaps they didn't even care enough to disbelieve him. Perhaps they ignored him altogether, which in many ways is much worse. In the same way the world will have little concern for the possibility that Jesus will return and judgement will come to the earth. They will be too busy eating or drinking or playing or sending e-mails or buying or selling or building or dreaming or singing, or doing just about anything but getting ready for the coming of the Lord. But make no mistake. That day is coming. Just as certainly as the flood came to Noah's generation, even so the Day of Judgement will come to the entire earth. And it may come sooner than anyone thinks.

1 Peter 3:18-21 is a fascinating passage that some scholars consider the most difficult to interpret in the New Testament. In just a few verses Peter connects Jesus, Noah, the flood, baptism, and the Resurrection. Here are his words: "For Christ died for sins once for all, the righteous for the unrighteous, to bring you to God. He was put to death in the body but made alive by the Spirit, through whom also he went and preached to the spirits in prison who disobeyed long ago when God waited patiently in the days of Noah while the ark was being built. In it only a few people, eight in all, were saved through water, and this water symbolises baptism that now saves you also—not the removal of dirt from the body but the pledge of a good conscience toward God. It saves you by the resurrection of Jesus Christ."

Though various interpretations are possible, Peter may be suggesting that the pre-incarnate Christ preached through Noah to his generation. Because they rejected his words, those unbelievers are the "spirits in prison" awaiting final judgement. In what sense do the floodwaters represent baptism "that now saves you also?" And in which sense did the floodwaters "save" Noah? The answer lies along these lines. The same waters that destroyed the world of that day also delivered Noah to a new world after the flood. Likewise, the waters of baptism deliver a believer from the old life of sin and destruction to a brand-new life.

Before we jump to the conclusion that water literally saves us, let's remember that not a drop of water actually touched Noah. He was saved "through" the water—that is, he passed through the flood—because he was in the ark. If he had literally been "in" the water, he would have perished with everyone else who died. It was the ark that saved him; the water merely delivered him from the old world to the new one. Peter is not teaching the idea that we are saved by baptism. It is Christ who saves by his death and his resurrection. Baptism is the pledge of a new believer whose conscience has been made clean by the blood of Christ. It is the believer's Pledge of Allegiance to the Lord who saved him. If the water symbolises baptism, then the ark must symbolise Jesus Christ. He is the "ark of salvation" to everyone who believes in him.

Consider these points of comparison: Just as the ark was provided by God, Christ was sent from heaven as a gracious provision for our salvation. The ark was sealed inside and out with "pitch." The Hebrew word for this resinous substance comes from the same root word translated elsewhere as "atonement" or "covering." Just as the pitch sealed and covered the spaces between the planks of gopher wood, the blood of Christ covers our sins so that they cannot rise up and condemn us any longer. There was only one ark provided and it had only one door. God never said, "Make four or five arks and let the people make their choice." And he never offered more than one door to the ark. Only one ark! Only one door! Jesus said, "I am the way, the truth and the life. No one comes to the Father except through me." The ark saved everyone who entered. And everyone who comes to Christ is saved. No one who comes to him in faith will be turned away.

Moreover, the ark was a place of total security. No matter how high the waters rose, the people and the animals inside were safe. Let the winds howl and the waves crash against the side. Let the rain fall for 40 days and 40 nights. It did not matter. The ark was so strong that it preserved everyone and everything inside. And those who come to Christ find that they are not only saved, they are safe forever and eternally secure. Once God shut the door, no one else could enter. This is a sad and solemn thought. While the door was open, anyone could enter and be saved from the coming flood. Once the door was shut, it would not be opened again until the flood was over. Today is the day of grace. The door of salvation is open to all who care to enter. Whosoever will may freely come. The invitation goes out to the entire world. God takes no delight in the death of the wicked. He delays the coming judgement that all may come to repentance. But the day of grace will not last forever.

Death comes to all men sooner or later. And there will come a time when the gospel call will end and judgement must begin. When the flood finally arrived, everyone inside the ark was saved while everyone outside perished in the rising waters. Perhaps some people came and banged on the door and cried, "Let us in!" When the floodwaters rose, the sceptics at last knew that Noah wasn't so crazy after all. But it was too late then. The same thing will happen when Christ returns to the earth. There will be a final separation between the saved and the lost.

Only one question remains. Are you in the Ark of Safety? I am not asking about your religion or your giving or your good works or your religious background. And I am not inquiring as to your baptism or your church membership or even about your Sunday attendance at Church. Those things are of small value when it comes to the issue of eternal destiny. If Christ is the ark, are you "in" Christ by faith? Or are you "outside" Christ because you have never trusted in him? I fear that many otherwise good and decent people (including some who may read this message) are hoping to "dog paddle" their way to heaven. They are not in the ark but they figure they can swim to safety if the need arises. But that's like saying, "I can swim from Dover to Cape Town." It can't be done. You're sure to drown and it doesn't matter how far you can swim. If you want to go to heaven, you must be in the ark. Jesus is the "Ark of Salvation." He alone can save you from your sins. He alone can deliver you to the shores of heaven. He alone can rescue you from the judgement to come. Run to the Ark! Run to the Ark of Salvation! Put your trust in Jesus Christ. May you and your family be found safe in the Ark of Salvation.

Chapter 3
Hope For Those Who Feel Forgotten
Genesis 7-8

The story of Noah is very exciting until you get to Genesis 7. At that point, the story seems to get bogged down in details. There is information about the various animals brought on board, and also a very specific accounting regarding the precise dates when certain events relating to the flood took place. It's easy to skim over this chapter and the next one in order to resume the "action" in Genesis 9. But that would be a great mistake. For one thing, it's hard to imagine any "action" greater than a world wide flood. These details are placed in the Bible for a reason. The Lord wants us to know what happened and how it happened, step by step.

Here's a brief summary of those details:

Noah entered the ark when he was 600 years, 2 months, and 10 days old.
Seven days later the rain began to fall. The rain fell for 40 days and 40 nights.
The "fountains of the great deep" (evidently subterranean caverns) also burst forth with water.
The floodwaters spread across the entire earth, covering the mountains to a depth of 20 feet.
All living creatures on dry land were wiped out.
The flood covered the earth for 150 days.
As the floodwaters receded, the ark came to rest on the mountains of Ararat, evidently the region of far eastern Turkey, near the border with Russia.
Seventy-four days later the tops of the mountains became visible.
Forty days later Noah sent out a raven.

Noah then sent out a dove on three occasions. The third time it did not return.

Two weeks later he saw dry land.

Noah stayed in the ark another 57 days until the Lord told him to leave.

Noah was 601 years, 2 months, and 27 days old when he left the ark.

If you add it all up, Noah spent one year and 17 days in the ark. That's a long time in a cramped space with lots and lots of animals. This was no luxury cruise. The ark was not equipped with a swimming pool. There were no movies, no entertainers, and no fancy buffets. There was nothing to do but stay in the boat while it floated aimlessly on the surface of the ocean. It was no picnic being on the ark.

The Bible does not tell us anything about Noah's personal emotions during the long time he spent in the ark. We know that he was a man of faith who took God at his Word. That's why he built the ark in the first place. However, he was human, too. The sea is a lonely place. It could not have been easy to be shut up inside the ark with his family and all those animals. Did he wonder if God had forgotten him? I could not blame him if he had his doubts.

He had done what God had said. He had preached to the unbelieving world. He had built the enormous ark. He led the animals two by two into the ark. He entered with his family. Now he is in a giant boat bobbing up and down with the waves. One day fades into another. He cannot see the sun because of the cloud cover. There is no course to follow, just drifting on the surface of the endless, endless ocean.

Have you ever felt abandoned by God?

Have you ever wondered if God has forgotten you? Have you ever felt as if your prayers were bouncing off the ceiling and hitting you on the head? If so, Genesis 8 is for you. The message of the chapter is given in verse 1: "But God remembered Noah and all the wild animals and the livestock that were with him in the ark, and he sent a wind over the earth, and the waters receded."

Consider that simple phrase: "God remembered Noah." Those three words tell us a great deal about the Lord. One of the greatest human fears is to be forgotten. We fear death because it means that ultimately we will be buried in a grave, the world will go on without us, and we will eventually be forgotten. If you doubt that, go to an old graveyard and study the tombstones of those who were buried in the early 1800s. Who are they? Where did they come from? What were they like? What did they do? And the greatest question: Does anyone today remember them? In most cases the answer is no. And if you go back far enough, you can find thousands of graves of forgotten people who lived and died and it is as if they were never here at all.

When the text tells us that God "remembered" Noah, it doesn't mean that God had forgotten him. It simply means that in the midst of the great flood, God stayed true to his promises. He promised to deliver Noah and his family and all those animals, and during the flood, with all its death and destruction, the Lord looked down on the earth and remembered to have mercy on eight people floating in a big barge with all those animals. Perhaps Noah felt forgotten by God. If so, he is in good company because the greatest saints of the ages have felt the same way. One man wrote of the "dark night of the soul" when he felt completely alone and abandoned by God.

The psalms are full of similar sentiments. Consider Psalm 42, "I say to God my Rock, 'Why have you forgotten me? Why must I go about mourning, oppressed by the enemy?' My bones suffer mortal agony as my foes taunt me, saying to me all day long, 'Where is your God?'" In the Lord Jesus we have the supreme example of the righteous man feeling abandoned. In his darkest moments on the cross, he cried out, "My God! My God! Why have you forsaken me?"

Our text contains an important message of hope. In the midst of judgement, God always remembers mercy. He remembers those who suffer and he keeps his eyes on them. Though they suffer long and often feel forgotten, the Almighty will not abandon them. As God remembered Noah, even so he will remember you and me. There is no trial so severe that it can separate us from the God who loves us.

How did God remember Noah? There were three ways in which the Lord remembered Noah during the flood.

(1) He sent a wind.

Genesis 8:1 is specific on this point. God sent a wind that blew across the whole earth and caused the floodwaters to begin to recede. This speaks of God's authority over the forces of nature. He commanded the wind and the wind blew. He said to the waters, "Settle down," and they settled down. At his command the water level began to decrease around the globe.

Proverbs 30 says that he holds the wind in his hands and wraps the waters in his cloak. According to Job 38, he puts limits on the waves and says to them, "Thus far and no farther you may go." Psalm 135 tells us that he brings wind out of the storehouses of heaven. Every drop of water, every gust of wind, and every tiny snowflake comes from the hands of God. Even hurricanes and tornadoes serve his purposes. The storms that batter the earth are fully under his divine control. Just as God has the key to open, he also has the key to shut. He turned off the faucet, the heavens dried up, and the water began to evaporate from the surface of the earth.

We should learn from this that when affliction has done its appointed work, it will be removed from us. Whether it be sickness or ill fortune or bad circumstances or hateful opposition or even truly bad weather, when God's purposes have been served, the hard times will go away. It is significant that the flood did not disappear in a day. The waters rose slowly and fell slowly. Even so, God usually works deliverance for us gradually, little by little, day by day, step by step. We don't get into trouble overnight and we don't get out of trouble overnight either.

(2) God gave Noah a sign.

Noah was looking for signs that the flood was coming to an end. I'm sure he was tired of being around those animals day and night. We can't even imagine the smells and the other aspects of living in the ark. No doubt Noah was ready to see the family have a little bit of elbowroom. It's not easy to dwell with your sons and your daughters-in-law and your wife in close range for over a year and, as one writer put it, you could never get out of the house and you could never get far enough away that you were out of trouble for whatever you had done wrong. I'm sure that Noah was ready to get out of that ark.

He sent out a raven. Since ravens feast on rotting flesh, it no doubt found plenty to eat on the surface of the ocean. It flew back and forth but did not return to the ark. The first time Noah sent out a dove, it came back because the water wasn't low enough. The second time the dove returned with an olive leaf, indicating that plants were beginning to grow. The third time he sent out a dove, it didn't come back at all. Noah knew then that the end of the flood must be very near.

Why did he send the birds in the first place? The answer is simple and perhaps easy to overlook. God had told him when the flood would start but not when it would end. He needed to know the approximate date it would begin so he could build the ark in time. But God never told him how long the flood would last because he didn't need to know. I think we can all relate to Noah's intention.

We can endure almost anything if only we know when it will end. That applies to sickness, personal pain, broken relationships, trouble at work, financial stress, or even watching our loved ones suffer. Whatever it is, we can take it if we know that two weeks from next Tuesday, our troubles will come to an end. Often, it is the not knowing that wears us down. We watch and wait and wonder and pray as the uncertainty gnaws away on the inside. Our chief question is always: "When will this end?" And the answer is always: "In God's time, not one day sooner, not one day later." Nothing can rush, change or hinder God's designs for his children. In our doubt and confusion, we rest on this truth: God can make the dry ground appear anytime he chooses. We may feel forgotten and abandoned in the flood, but the dry land will appear in due time.

Notice also that Noah didn't get out of the ark for a long time even after the first land appeared. I think after a year on the ark, I would have jumped over the side and started for the shore as soon as the first peak poked through the surface of the water. But Noah still had lots of waiting to do. This should not surprise us. In the course of life, God often delays his mercies in order that we should properly thank him when they finally appear.

We pray, "Lord, help us," and the next day we pray again, "Lord, have mercy," and the next day we cry out, "Lord, hear our prayers." Sometimes we are compelled to pray the same prayer for many days or weeks or months or years. All of this is for our ultimate benefit. His answers are delayed in order that his sovereignty might be established (He's God and we're not), and that our hearts might be humbled, and to ensure that when the answer finally comes, he alone gets the glory. In our haste (or frustration or desperation) we may try to leave the ark too soon. We may try to unhinge the door or climb out through the window or even knock a hole in the side of the ark. But when we do, we slip and slide through the mud and end up in the water. It is better that we should wait for God's answers to appear, and to trust that our Heavenly Father will give us what we need when we need it.

Just as God gave Noah a sign, he still gives signs and tokens of his grace today. Often it is a Scripture or a song repeated at just the right moment. Or a phone call or a letter that came when we felt like giving up. God does not always spare us the pain of life, but he gives us tokens, roses that bloom in the snow, to remind us that even in our sadness and even in our despair, we are never alone, never forgotten.

(3) God spoke to him again.

The final way God remembered Noah was by speaking to him again. In verses 16-17 the Lord instructed Noah to leave the ark with his family and the animals. As far as we can tell, this is the first time God had spoken to Noah since he told him to enter the ark. The year in between had been a time of silence from heaven. What a long year it must have been inside the ark with the boat drifting aimlessly on the waters. As Noah watched and waited, he went about his duties, wondering when the Lord would speak to him again. Who could blame him if he felt forgotten? The same thing can happen to any of us. You may come to a time in your life when you feel forgotten and alone. You may think that the heavens have become as brass and that your prayers are bouncing back at you. You may lack the conscious sense of God's presence so that you feel abandoned and left to face life on your own.

What do you do then? You must do what Noah did. Stay faithful to what you know to be true. Obey the Lord and follow the light that you were given in the past. Day after day, Noah had to get up and take care of his responsibilities on the ark. It did not matter if he "felt" like it or not. God had given him a job to do and it must be done. His feelings did not matter. He knew that God had led him this far, and he believed that God had his best interests at heart. While he waited for the Lord to speak again, he did the only thing he could do. He remained faithful.

Do not doubt in the darkness what God has shown you in the light. Wait on the Lord. And while you wait, obey as much as you know. When the time comes, God will speak to you again. You can't rush God. In his time, you will hear his voice once again. Until that day comes, stay faithful. Do your duty. There is no reason to stay in bed and mope. Get up and do what must be done. God will speak to you in due time.

Although Genesis 8 is primarily about God remembering Noah, it also contains wonderful truth about how Noah remembered God. Over 300 years ago, Matthew Henry offered this comment: "Those that remember God, shall certainly be remembered by Him, no matter how desolate their condition." Our text reveals two specific ways in which Noah remembered the Lord.

(1) He left the Ark.

"So Noah came out, together with his sons and his wife and his sons' wives. All the animals and all the creatures that move along the ground and all the birds—everything that moves on the earth—came out of the ark, one kind after another."

I do not think we appreciate how much courage it took for Noah to leave the ark. As I have already pointed out, the ark had been crowded, cramped, and no doubt somewhat smelly. But it has been home, and it was safe. Now they were leaving the known for the unknown. The world they had known was gone forever. Cities gone, roads gone, homes gone, people gone. Geography changed, landmarks all different. Nothing looked the same. Everything was new. It might have been easier to stay in the ark, uncomfortable though it was. It took great courage to step out of the ark into a brand-new world. It meant leaving behind safety and security. And it meant trusting God for a totally unknown future.

Sometimes—often!—God calls us to do things that are hard and may even seem impossible. We are called to leave the known for the unknown, and we have to leave the ark that has taken us this far and step out on our own. It's scary and unnerving and harrowing because once we leave the familiar confines, we can never go back there again. To leave the ark meant embarking on a new life with new dangers and new opportunities. That takes courage and resolve and a decision not to look back or to second-guess yourself.

Noah and his family came out first. That wasn't easy either. If it had been me, I think I would have sent out the tigers or the lions first. Maybe I would have slapped one of the elephants on the rump and said, "Okay, big fellow. Get out and look around." Noah led the way and his family followed. That took courage as well. If things went bad, he would have to deal with it.

Faith means taking the next step … and then trusting God with the results. It is a paradox of life that even though the ark is smelly and cramped, we may be afraid to leave it because it represents the only security we have known. Sometimes we pray for a change in our circumstances, but when the moment comes, we are so overwhelmed with fear that we are paralysed and unable to move.

Perhaps we should add a verse to Hebrews 11. By faith Noah built the ark; by faith Noah entered the Ark; by faith Noah left the ark. Which was harder? To enter the ark or to leave it? Both can be very difficult. Some of us are stuck because we know it's time to move forward but we are afraid to take the first step. God bless Noah who knew when to get on the big boat and he also knew when to get off!

(2) Noah built an Altar.

"Then Noah built an altar to the Lord and, taking some of all the clean animals and clean birds, he sacrificed burnt offerings on it." The sequence of events is very important. God tells Noah to leave the ark, he leaves the ark, and the first thing he does after stepping on dry ground is to build an altar to the Lord. Not many people would have done that as their first act after getting out of the ark.

I can imagine most folks running from the ark, kicking up their heels, and saying, "Let's go. Let's get started. We've got a world to build. Let's not waste time." Not Noah. His first act was to publicly thank God for his deliverance. Like the ten lepers who were cured by Jesus and only one returned to give thanks, even so we often receive great blessings from the Lord and in our haste to enjoy them, we seldom stop to say thanks.

Noah took time to build an altar and make sacrifices to the Lord. The offering represented his complete surrender and total dedication to the Lord. After the flood Noah could see that God was not only a God of wrath, but also a God of mercy.

Noah recognised that he owed everything to the Lord. It was God who warned him, God who told him to build the ark, God who designed the ark, God who called the animals to the ark two by two, God who shut the door, God who preserved the ark through the flood, God who brought the ark to a safe place, and it was God who told Noah when it was safe to leave the ark. God did it all! Noah was just along for the ride!

This is an Old Testament picture of salvation by grace alone. Noah added nothing to the equation. (Even the strength and perseverance to build the ark came from God.) Noah takes no credit but by his offering signifies that God has delivered him and his family. His offering is a way of saying, "By rights I should have perished in that flood but God in his mercy delivered me."

What a challenge this is for all of us to "remember God" in all that we do. As Ecclesiastes puts it: "Remember your Creator in the days of your youth." We are to remember God in our early days while we have strength and energy and all of life stretches out before us. If we remember God in our youth, we are less likely to forget him when we are old.
In your youth … Remember God!
In your marriage … Remember God!
In your singleness … Remember God!
In your victories and in your defeats … Remember God!
In your joys and in your sorrows … Remember God!
In your sickness and in your health … Remember God!
In your old age … Remember God!
In your dying moments … Remember God!

Jeremiah 51:50 instructs us to "remember the Lord in a distant land." In its original setting, these words applied to the Jewish exiles that had been taken from their homeland in Judah and carried into captivity in Babylon. They were now far from home, in a new culture, surrounded by people who did not share their faith, facing every day the twin temptations of despair and compromise. How would they survive? The answer is clear. Don't forget your God! Remember who you are and whose you are. Remember where you came from! Remember the Lord who is with you even now, in your anguish and in your humiliation. This is a good word for today. The "distant land" for some Christians means that you are far removed from family and friends. Some of you have moved from a safe secure environment to where you now are.

Perhaps you are starting a new job or have moved to a new neighbourhood. Perhaps you have just got married or perhaps you are single again. Life has suddenly changed! The familiar patterns of life have disappeared and now everything is different. You are cut off from your roots. Beware! This is a time of enormous spiritual danger. Do not listen to the whisper of the devil when he says, "Don't worry about it. No one back home will know. Your so-called friends have forgotten you."

Remember the Lord in a distant land!
Remember the Lord who saved you.
Remember the Lord who forgave you.
Remember the Lord who loves you.
Remember the Lord who is with you even now.

Now is the time to remember God.

Let this be your motto: *I will remember the Lord.*
Take time to give thanks.
Build an altar where you will meet the Lord every day.
Take time to pray.
Speak up for Jesus.
Bless the name of the Lord—and do it publicly.

Remember the God who remembers you. He will be your joy and comfort in this life and in the life to come.

Every time I hear about Noah's Ark, I think of Bill Cosby. Have any of you heard his bit on Noah? Well, there were actually three parts to that. The one you're most familiar with involves the exchange between Noah and the Lord. The second part is the exchange between Noah and his neighbour. His neighbour is giving Noah grief about getting that boat out of his driveway so he can get to work. When the neighbour asks for a hint as to what the ark is for, Noah replies, "How long can you tread water?" Finally in another conversation between Noah and the Lord, Noah loses it. He starts ranting and yelling at God, telling him he's letting all the animals go and he's burning the ark down. God asks Noah, "How long can you tread water?" Cosby's version is totally fictional, and totally wrong, of course. Noah may have been ridiculed by his neighbours but nothing in scripture implies that he ever argued with or yelled at God about his task. Noah was a man of faith who was obedient to God, even though he couldn't possibly see the outcome.

The African Impala can jump to a height of over 10 feet and cover a distance of more than 30 feet. Yet they're kept in a zoo caged in with a 3 ft. wall. The animals will not jump if they can't see where their feet will fall. They won't jump if they can't see the outcome. Too many of us are like that. We're shut down by a 3-foot wall. Just because we can't see the other side, we won't jump. It takes faith to leap over that wall. Noah had this faith and obedience. You can't spend 120 years building a 450 ft. long, 75 ft. wide, and 45 ft. high boat in the middle of a desert without faith and obedience.

Finally, it happens. The clouds and thunder and water come. Can you imagine what it must have been like when people, realising what had happened, began to bang on the sides. Noah and his family, it tells us in chapter 7, verse 16, have been safely locked inside by the hand of God. Noah had done what he could. God used Noah to try and reach those that had turned their backs on God and His ways. The people had 120 years to change but they refused to listen.

The story of Noah's Ark is a good one, but it's more than just a kid's story of animals two by two. It's also a story about God using ordinary, everyday people with faith. And God is still using people like that today.

He won't ask us to build an Ark in our backyard but he does still call us to be faithful. He may call us to reach out to people that make us uncomfortable. He may call us to take a risk financially in order to reach others. He may call us to do something no one has ever done before. He may call us to care for someone who won't appreciate it. He may call us to love someone we consider unlovable. Most of all, He will call us to show faith and follow where He leads.

God can use you to do what you never thought possible. Just because you've failed in the past doesn't mean that God can't use you now. God is looking for someone to leap over that three-foot wall. He's looking for someone with the faith of Noah. Someone willing to simply do what He says. Are you willing to do that? Are you willing to do things God's way rather than your own? Are you willing to trust Him rather than yourself? Over and over God uses ordinary people. He's calling you. He will use you . . . if you'll let Him.

Chapter 4
Judgement First, Then Mercy
Genesis 9:1-17

We're well on our way through the incredible days of Noah. This story is so familiar that we may miss the importance of what God asked of Noah. Noah was asked to build a vessel that was four and a half stories high and as long as a football field and a half - even though he lived over 500 miles from any water! And according to some scholars, it had never rained before upon the earth at that time. So, here we have people who are totally unfamiliar with water coming from the sky, or floods, and Noah is building a big ship to float away in. Can you imagine how Noah explained that one to people? Not only did God ask Noah to build this great vessel for which there was no precedent, he had to do so in the midst of public ridicule. Certainly, others must have known him as "crazy Noah". I wouldn't be surprised if families travelling on vacation would make it a point to drive by and see the man who was building something "God told him to build". How do you think that scenario would be played out if it happened today? Let's take a look and see.

The Lord spoke to Noah and said: "I'm going to make it rain until the whole earth is covered with water and all the evil people will be destroyed. But I will save you and your family, and two of every kind of living thing on the planet. I am ordering you to build Me an Ark." And God gave Noah the specifications for an Ark. "OK," said Noah, trembling in fear and fumbling with the blueprints. Then the Lord said, "Six months, and it starts to rain, so you'd better get a move on, Noah."

Six months passed. The skies began to cloud up and rain began to fall. The Lord saw that Noah was sitting in his front yard, just looking at this huge stack of lumber. But the Lord saw no Ark. The Lord shouted, "Noah! Where is my Ark?" "Lord, please forgive me!" begged Noah. "I did my best. But there were big problems. First I had to get a building permit for the Ark's construction, and your plans didn't meet the local fire code. So I had to hire an engineer to redraw the plans. Then, my neighbours objected, claiming I was violating zoning by building the Ark in my front yard, so I had to get a variance from the city planning commission. Then I had a big problem getting enough wood for the Ark because there was a ban on cutting trees in order to save some kind of owl. I had to convince Fish and Wildlife people that I needed the wood to save the owls. But they wouldn't let me catch any owls. Then the carpenters formed a union and went out on strike. I had to negotiate with them before anyone would pick up a saw or a hammer.

When I started gathering up animals, an animal rights group sued me. Then, the government got involved and wanted to know where I got the money for the lumber. Now I'm trying to resolve a complaint from the Equal Employment Opportunity Commission over how many people I'm supposed to hire. And on top of all that the Tax Man seized all my assets claiming I'm trying to avoid paying taxes by leaving the country.

Noah's society was corrupt, and so is ours today. And all during this time of building, Noah is preaching to the people. He preached but no one responded. But Noah continued doing what God called him to do. He trusted God's Word and God's promise. And that's what made him a man of faith.

Think about what happened as a result of this one man. Noah was able to save his family, and because of what he did, he saved humanity itself! I want you to notice that Noah was able to accomplish all this, not because he was overly capable or overly smart – but he was faithful enough to do what God wanted him to do.

I want you to understand that this is not just a story about what happened long ago. God is still using individuals today to do

His work. He may not ask you to build an Ark in your front yard, but He will call you to be faithful to Him. He may ask you to take a financial risk in order to reach others. There have been many people over the years that have come to your church needing cash, and there have been many who have answered the door who have dug into their own wallets to meet that need. He might ask you to do things for Him when others fight against it, and He might ask you to let someone falsely accuse you, and then to show them nothing but love in return, because you are more concerned with what they feel than what you feel. He may even ask you to pick up your cross and follow Him – even if you have to move away and leave everyone you love and every thing you find comfortable.

My wife Pauline and I have moved several times and it's been hard to do, but something that you never think about not doing. As hard as it is to do that, it is one of the most fulfilling blessings a person can have in life. If God ever calls you to "go and do", my encouragement to you is to simply "GO AND DO". One person can make a difference. You can make a difference; if you will let God use you. But you must remember some things. Remember that God is not looking for perfection or talent. He is looking for willing hearts. God does not call the qualified – He qualifies the called. Before God can use you for His kingdom, you must be *F.A.T.* You must be *Faithful* in following Him. You must be *Available* to follow Him. And, you must be *Teachable* so you can follow Him. God will put the opportunities in front of those who are willing to accept them. But there is always a sacrifice involved. To step forward for God, you must be willing to step out of where you are now. You cannot stand in one spot and move forward, can you? God is looking for those who will dare to trust Him as Noah did; someone willing to do what He says to do. I personally think it is time that we start letting God use us, because we have all used Him too long. When we decide to let God guide us, it is not a decision to be made lightly. It is the deepest of commitments. God is not looking for the weak; He is looking for that which is solid and strong. He is not looking for those who will talk loudly, but those who will talk boldly. He is just looking for ordinary people who are willing to trust in a very great God.

I just want to add here that there is strong historical evidence supporting the flood. Do you know that archaeologists have discovered 250 different flood legends from 250 different ancient cultures. There are 33 primary ancient cultures that have been discovered. 33 of 33 have a flood tradition. 31 of 33 have a common tradition that the flood was globally destructive. 32 of 33 say man was somehow divinely saved in the flood. 30 of 33 say there was some kind of special provision made for the animals. 25 of 33 describe an ark or boat landing on top of a mountain. 29 of 33 describe a bird being sent from the boat to find land. 30 of 33 describe a coloured arch as a symbol of divine favour. 31 of 33 say the first thing the people did when they landed on dry ground was to worship God. I should think so!

Let's suppose you are a reporter assigned by your editor to cover Noah's flood. It's the biggest story of the ancient world, and it's your story. So you research it and you write it up. When it's done, you turn it in, the editor reads it, and pays you the ultimate compliment, "Let's run this on page one." Then he asks a question you haven't thought about. "What's the headline?" You pause, considering the question carefully. After all, the flood has so many angles, so many amazing parts to it. How will you sum it all up in just a few gripping words?

Hold that thought for just a moment. A few years ago a panel of distinguished rabbis, pastors and scholars from various fields were invited on a television programme to discuss the contemporary meaning of the events recorded in Genesis. When they came to the episode about the flood, the panel was asked the same question I just asked: What headline would you write if you were covering the great flood of Noah's day? One panellist suggested this headline: *"God Destroys World in Flood."* Another panellist, a pastor, suggested something completely different: *"God Gives Humans a Second Chance."* Who was closer to the truth? From one standpoint, the first headline was biblically and historically accurate. God did destroy the world with a flood. That's a fact. It's also a very eye-catching headline. Probably not many of us would have thought of the second suggestion about God giving humans a second chance. It doesn't catch the drama of the ark, the flood, and the death of a civilisation. And it's not nearly as exciting. But on a very deep level, it does bring us to the bottom line of the story. After the floodwaters receded, after the animals left the ark, and after Noah and his family stood on dry land again, God did indeed give humanity a second chance.

That is the message we find in Genesis 9. Once the flood is over, Noah and his family have the task of starting all over again. Going through this passage, keep in mind that it's all about God. He's the only person who speaks or acts. Noah doesn't say a thing and he doesn't do a thing. God is the subject, the actor, the initiator. He establishes a new beginning, puts forth a new command, and gives a new promise. If we pay attention, we will discover vital principles regarding the possibility of spiritual renewal in every age and in any situation. "Then God blessed Noah and his sons, saying to them, 'Be fruitful and increase in number and fill the earth. The fear and dread of you will fall upon all the beasts of the earth and all the birds of the air, upon every creature that moves along the ground, and upon all the fish of the sea; they are given into your hands. Everything that lives and moves will be food for you. Just as I gave you the green plants, I now give you everything'."

If the first verse sounds familiar, that's because it's a repeat of what God said to Adam and Eve in Genesis 1:28. This is Eden all over again. God commissions Noah and his family to spread out across the earth and re-establish human civilisation. Noah is to become the patriarch of a vast clan that will eventually branch out to form all the various tribes and nations on earth. Just as Adam was head of the human race in the beginning, Noah is now the head of the reconstituted human race after the flood. Everything flows from him through his three sons. And now God adds one significant permission. Humans are given permission to use animals for food. Evidently before the flood, everyone was a vegetarian. But now it is permissible to hunt animals for food and to raise animals for meat.

There is a vital spiritual truth underlying these verses. God will not be defeated by human sin, not even by sin as gross as the immorality that brought on the flood. Your sin may seem (from a human point of view) to hinder God's plan, it may seem to delay it for days or months or years or even for generations, but in the end, God's will is going to be done. What God has spoken must come to pass. No evil done by men can thwart the plans of the Almighty. Has he not spoken? Will he not do it? Who dares to stand against him? Some may dare, but none can succeed. This truth is hugely encouraging because it gives us hope when we have messed up royally. We may wonder, and may secretly think, that God is through with us because of our sin. "I've sinned too much. God will never give me another chance." Those who say that know too much about their sin and too little about their God.

Isaiah 55:7 contains a wonderful invitation to those who feel their sin is too great to be forgiven: "Let the wicked forsake his way and the evil man his thoughts. Let him turn to the Lord, and he will have mercy on him, and to our God, for he will freely pardon." The King James translates the last phrase—"he will abundantly pardon." I like that because that's precisely what I need. When I stray, when I fall, when I make a mess of my life, I need a God who will "abundantly" pardon me. With God there is always the possibility of a new beginning.

"But you must not eat meat that has its lifeblood still in it. And for your lifeblood I will surely demand an accounting. I will demand an accounting from every animal. And from each man, too, I will demand an accounting for the life of his fellow man. Whoever sheds the blood of man, by man shall his blood be shed; for in the image of God has God made man. As for you, be fruitful and increase in number; multiply on the earth and increase upon it."

In these verses Noah now learns the "rules of the game." If God is going to start over again, Noah needs to know what rules to follow. These verses tell us there is basically only one rule—"Respect Life." Everything flows from that. That rule is applied in two sub-rules.

(1) Don't eat living animals.

That's the meaning of verse 4, which sounds strange to our ears. In order to understand it, we should perhaps add the word "pulsating" after the word "lifeblood." Since God now gives permission to eat animals for food, he adds the restriction that they must first be put to death and the blood drained from them. This would seem to be good advice in any case. It's very difficult to eat a steak while it is still attached to a living cow. And even harder to eat living pork chops. This text anticipates the later biblical instruction that the life of the flesh is in the blood.

The blood carries the pulse of life. When Medics arrive at the scene of an accident, one of the first things they do is to check for a pulse. If they get a pulse, they know the person is alive. The point of first killing the animal, draining the blood, and then eating it is to show respect for God who gave life in the first place.

(2) Murderers should be put to death.

This is the plain meaning of verses 5-6. If a man sheds the blood of another man, by the hand of man his own blood will be shed. Life for life. If you kill, you will be killed. If you murder, you will be put to death. If you show such disrespect for human life that you murder it, then you have forfeited your right to your own life.

The reason given for this rule is crucial. Verse 6 says it is because man is made in the image of God. Think about what that means. Everyone we know, everyone we meet, everyone in the whole world is made in the image of God. To put it stronger, God made each one of us in his own image. He stamped all of us and each of us with his divine image. We were each created with the ability to know God, to love him, and to serve him. We were made with an inner desire to know our Creator. That separates us forever from the dogs and cats and mules and robins and beetles and rabbits and whales and gophers and chimpanzees. Those creatures are creatures. Nothing more and nothing less. But humans are made in God's image. That makes each one of us unique and valuable and worthy of respect and honour and protection. And that image of God means that human life is valuable inside the womb, from the very moment of conception.

How dare anyone murder another person made in God's image? If you do, God takes it seriously. He will not forget it or overlook it or excuse it or pass it off as a dumb mistake. And he won't say, "Boys will be boys" or "She deserved it" or "Let's all be friends." No! God says, "If you murder, you deserve to die."

This is the biblical foundation for capital punishment. We all understand that God is the source of life. He alone has the right to give life or to take it away. But in this passage God delegates to human authority the right to take life in certain circumstances. Later on in the Old Testament God will specify certain circumstances where the death penalty is justified. The death penalty was prescribed for murder, working on the Sabbath, cursing your father or mother, adultery, rape and kidnapping. It should be observed that each of these crimes constitutes an assault on God's Law, or on one of God's institutions (such as marriage and the family), or upon a person created in God's image.

To discuss this issue in depth would take an entire book, but suffice it to say that I am not aware of any passage in the rest of the Bible that contradicts, cancels and nullifies what is said in Genesis 9. The principle laid down thousands of years ago is still in force today. Romans 13:4 tells us that when a civil authority (judge, police officer, soldier, etc) acts to uphold righteousness and to punish evildoers, he does not bear the sword in vain. That sword of punishment—which includes capital punishment—is part of God's judgement against those who do evil, and especially against those who take innocent human life. If you ask me, "Would I like to see Capital Punishment back on the law books in my country." The answer would be, 'No!' I think we have moved a long way from the general biblical standards set out for a new nation in the Bible. These are debatable points and I don't want us getting away from the main message. People made in the image of God are to be valued very highly indeed. That's the main point.

God made a wonderful promise at this time of new beginnings. If you attended Sunday School as a child, you already know the promise and the sign. God promised never again to flood the entire earth. God placed a rainbow in the sky as the sign of his promise. In theological terms, this is the first great covenant of the Bible, the Noahic Covenant. It is important for several reasons.

It is an unconditional covenant.

There are no conditions to be met by us. God didn't say, "If you obey me, I promise never to flood the earth again," or "If you offer a sacrifice, I promise never to flood the earth again." To the contrary, God asks nothing of the human race. No obedience, no sacrifice, no faith, no prayer. Nothing at all. This isn't a two-way street where we do something and then God does something in response. This is a promise made by God in spite of the fact that the world had just been destroyed because of sin, and in full knowledge that the world was soon to plunge back into the pit of sin and that it will be Noah the man of faith who will later lead the parade in the wrong direction. This is a covenant of pure grace, made in spite of human sin, not because of any supposed human goodness or human faith or human obedience. In spite of our continuing sin, God promises never again to destroy the entire human race with a flood. Pure, free grace greater than our sin.

It is a covenant guaranteed with a sign.

We have tended to sentimentalise this part of the story, and for good reason. Rainbows are beautiful, and it's easy to think that this is just a sweet touch. But it's far more than that. Rainbows occur all over the world, thus making the sign available to the same extent as the flood itself. Rainbows are a startling phenomenon. When you see a rainbow, the natural urge is to point it out to someone else. Rainbows display their colours across the full spectrum of light, covering all possible shades and hues. Here is a sign perfectly fitted for the entire human race, at all times, in every location. And it is a sign easily understood by all ages. The text tells us that when we see a rainbow, we are to think, "God promised never again to send a flood upon the entire earth." And when God sees a rainbow, it reminds him of the promise he freely made to us.

Think about this rainbow promise. Notice that nowhere does God say, "I will never send a storm again." Nowhere does God promise that life will be free of storms, trials, troubles and difficulties. Most rainbows appear only after the storm has come and gone. If there were no storms, there would be very few rainbows.

The message to us is important.

God never promises a life free from pain and suffering. As the song says, he never promised us a rose garden. Or if he did, the roses have thorns. That's life in a fallen world. There are floods and fires and tornadoes. And there are wars and famines and terrorist attacks. We are all aware that this is not a safe world, that we all live on the front lines, and that evil is all around us. No one is immune from disease. Bad news is only a phone call away. The rainbows come after the rain, not before. Weeping endures for a night, joy comes in the morning. We know that all things work together for good, and we know that the "all things" must include tears and suffering, unanswered questions, and moments of anger, terror and sadness. Even when we quote those famous words of Joseph in Genesis 50:20, when he tells his brothers, "You meant it for evil but God meant it for good," we must realise that you can't get to the last phrase without going through the first phrase. I take from this a familiar truth. God will give us more than we can bear, but never more than He can bear as He sustains us. The human race can't bear another world wide flood so God won't send one. And the rainbow proves his promise. But there will still be many storms along the way, tears aplenty, and much sadness. And if we look up, we will see God's rainbows, the signs and tokens of his love, here and there along the way, reminding us that the storms of life do not mean that things are out of control. The rainbow teaches us that everything is under God's control.

Standing back and looking at this passage from a distance, the last phrase of Habakkuk 3:2 comes to mind. It's a prayer by the prophet as he considers the suffering of his own people. Although they have sinned greatly and their judgement is deserved, he prays that it will come to an end. He frames his thoughts in a few simple words: "In wrath remember mercy." Perhaps that is a good summary of this passage. In wrath God remembered mercy. In wrath God always remembers mercy. When he judges, it is to purify and to discipline, not to destroy. And sooner or later, his mercy will be seen. And it is after the wrath is over that his mercy is most clearly displayed.

The 'headline' question.

The more I think about it, the more I like the headline that says, *"God Gives Humans a Second Chance."* I like it because that's what Genesis 9 is all about. And I like it because that's what we need. Come to think of it, I like it because that's what I need. I need that second chance every day. Judgement and wrath, times of hardship and difficulty. Yes. A second chance. Yes! The rainbow after the rain. Yes! In wrath God always remembers mercy.

The judgement and the mercy both come from God.

It's not as if the devil sent the flood but God sent the rainbow. Oh no. God himself sent the terrible judgement of the flood. He is the one who sent the rain and opened up the fountains of the deep. He is the one who ordained that the world of that day should perish. He is the one who after the flood showed his mercy in giving the human race a second chance and in making the promise and guaranteeing it with a rainbow.

Without the judgement, the mercy would not appear as merciful.

The rainbow is always beautiful, but the promise is more glorious because of the flood that preceded it. Three times God says, "Never again!" He really meant it. Never again will there be a world wide flood. Mercy is still mercy but mercy shines ever brighter, like a diamond set against black velvet, when seen against the backdrop of God's righteous judgement. The application moves in many directions, all of them encouraging to us.

There is a word here to *backsliders*. That's an old word, isn't it? A backslider is a Christian who has drifted away from the Lord. You love the Lord but the cares of this world and the temptations of life have put you in a bad place, far from the conscious presence of God. Perhaps you feel so frustrated that you wonder if things can ever be different. Here is good news. If you will return to the Lord, the clouds will part, the sun will shine, and overhead you will find the rainbow of God's mercy. Why live in the "far country" of sin when you as a child of God can feast at the Father's table?

There is good news for *sinners*. Your sin, no matter what it is, has already been judged. The Day of Judgement happened 2,000 years ago when Jesus died on the cross for you. His blood is so powerful that it paid in full the price for all your sins.

Your sins were judged at the cross. Today is the day of mercy. Come to the cross. Or better still, run to the cross!
"Mercy there was great and grace was free,
Pardon there was multiplied to me,
There my burdened soul found liberty,
At Calvary."

62

It is no coincidence that when John saw the vision of heaven in Revelation 4, he saw a rainbow encircling the throne of God. That symbolises the completeness of God's mercy. The blood of Jesus has transformed the throne of God from a throne of judgement into a throne of mercy. The rainbow promise guarantees that God's mercy is for you. For all of us who labour under heavy burdens and deep personal sorrows, this promise is for us, too. Look up and you will see the rainbow, the sign that God has not forgotten you.

Chapter 5
The Problem Of Racism
Genesis 9:18-10:32

It's impossible to talk about Genesis 9:18 to the end of chapter 10 without considering the problem of *racism*. Although, if you come to this text with no prior history and no preconceptions, you may wonder about the connection between this strange story of drunkenness, nakedness, family trouble and the curse on Canaan and the problem of race relations in the 21st century. That is true because this text, while fascinating and perhaps even a bit strange, seems to offer very little that would apply to issues of prejudice, hatred and racial discrimination. As is so often the case in studying the Bible, there is more to this story than meets the eye. Historically, this text is important because for a long time certain groups used it to justify slavery and segregation. Lurking underneath this misinterpretation was the belief that people should be treated differently on the basis of skin colour and racial origin. As a result, the curse on Canaan was misused in support of an ugly doctrine of racial superiority.

This teaching, which was once very popular in western churches, has thankfully almost totally disappeared. Yet racism and prejudice remain with us today. And if we go back to the New Testament, we discover that the early church struggled with these same issues as Jewish and Gentile believers tried to find a way to live together in the same congregations. It is still a problem in the Christian church. When I was a Church Pastor in Manchester I would look out at the congregation on a Sunday morning and it looked like a mini- United Nations to me. We had folks from all around the world worshipping with us. What should we say about the changing face of our own church?

First, this is a very good thing. Second, it is likely to continue in the years to come. There is no turning the clock back, even if we wanted to, which we don't. Having said that, there is also the reality that growing diversity brings its own set of problems. It's easy for a church to fragment into competing groups that bicker over issues large and small. The challenge is for believers from various backgrounds to affirm their own heritage while not looking down on others who may be different in many ways. This is not always easy to do but that makes the challenge all the more important.

As we come to the text, we can break it down into two parts:

Noah's Nakedness – verses 18-23.
Noah's Curse – verses 24-29.

Soon after the flood Noah planted a vineyard. When the grapes were ripe, he picked them and made wine. Then he got drunk from the wine and ended up naked in his tent. At some point his youngest son, Ham, saw him passed out in the tent, naked. The Hebrew text suggests that Ham stared at his father or perhaps leered at him. There is a suggestion of indecency in what he did. Ham then told his two older brothers, Shem and Japheth, what he had seen. Evidently he thought it was funny and meant to hold up his father to ridicule. The brothers didn't see it that way at all. They were shocked at the news and knew they needed to cover their father's nakedness. So they took a garment (the Hebrew text says "the garment," perhaps meaning that it was Noah's own blanket) and held it at their shoulders, walking backward while they covered their father, lest they should see his nakedness. When Noah woke up, he found out what Ham had done. Perhaps the two brothers told him about it. At that point the story takes an unexpected turn. Noah pronounces a curse upon Canaan, Ham's youngest son. In a sense, it is a just punishment. Just as his youngest son had dishonoured him, now Ham's youngest son will pay the price. Noah prophesies that he will become a "slave of slaves" to his three brothers and also to Shem and Japheth.

Here's a shorter version of that story. Noah got drunk, got naked, and passed out in his tent. Ham saw it, told his brothers; they refused to look, and covered their father. Noah wakes up and pronounces a curse not on Ham but on Ham's son Canaan, prophesying slavery for him and ultimately for his descendants.

Here's an even shorter version. Noah got drunk. Ham showed disrespect to his father. Noah woke up and pronounced a curse on his grandson, Canaan.

Even faster . . . Father gets drunk. Son takes advantage. Grandson is cursed.

This is certainly a very strange story . . .

1) Noah was a man of faith who did great things for God, yet in a moment of weakness he got drunk. His sin starts the ball rolling in the wrong direction. Sometimes smart people can do very dumb things. And they often hurt others in the process. Usually it's the people closest to them who get hurt the most.

2) This is the first mention of wine in the Bible, and it leads to nakedness, exposure, humiliation, and family trouble. There is a warning here for anyone who cares to take it. Later in the Bible the Old Testament prophets will make explicit the connection between drunkenness, nakedness and immorality.

3) There is a warning here about the dangers of nakedness. To most of us the fact that Ham saw his father naked doesn't seem like such a big deal. But that says more about us than it does about the Bible. Modesty and decency and not exposing yourself to others—these are moral values that accompany holiness.

Our great problem today is that we have almost no sense of identification with the attitudes or actions of Noah's two godly sons, Shem and Japheth. We feel no shame and no shock at the report of Noah inside his tent. The reason is the real shock of the passage: We are a part of a society that senses no shame and no shock at moral and sexual indecency. Virtually every kind of sexual intimacy is portrayed on the cinema and television screen. Even abnormal and perverted conduct has become routine to us. Without any sense of indecency the most intimate and private items are advertised before us and our children. Do you see the point? We are not troubled by Noah's nakedness because we are so much farther down the path of decadence that we hardly flinch at what happened in this passage.

If the condemnation of God fell upon Ham's actions and upon those who walked in his ways, what does that say to you and to me? God forgive us for our lack of *shock-ability* and shame. God save us from the sins of the Canaanites. May God teach us to value moral purity and to be ruthless with sin. May we refuse to let it live among us, just as Israel was taught in this text.

4) Ham's greatest sin was in taking advantage of his father's weakness. A good son would have protected his father, not spread the news to his brothers. Ham broke the 5th Commandment—Honour your Father and Mother. By telling his brothers, he dishonoured his father and brought shame to his name. No son should ever do that for any reason.

5) Shem and Japheth showed a different spirit by refusing even to look on their father's nakedness. No doubt they were embarrassed and wanted only to protect their father.

Crucial questions arise about Noah's response.

Was he acting in anger and was his anger justified? The text does not specifically say that Noah was angry so we can't answer the first part with certainty. I know I would be angry if one of my children did to me what Ham did to Noah. If Noah was angry, he was justified. Dishonouring your parents is a serious sin, not to be taken lightly.

Did Noah have the power to literally curse his grandson? Yes, but only if God backed him up. That is, Noah could say anything he liked—a blessing, a promise, a curse, a threat—but none of it would matter unless God backed it up. In this case, Noah was reflecting God's judgement, not just his own.

Why did Noah curse his grandson Canaan and not his son Ham? The text does not fully answer that question. It's possible that Canaan was somehow involved in Ham's sinful disrespect. The key to understanding the curse is to remember that Canaan became the father of a vast group of people called the Canaanites. In later generations they occupied the land of Israel (called Canaan) and developed an idolatrous religion based on gross sexual perversion. Leviticus 18 specifies the sins of the Canaanites in graphic detail.

As we consider Genesis 9, it's important for us to see the connection. Ham was the father of Canaan and Canaan was the father of the Canaanites. The Canaanites were sexually perverted idol-worshipers who were the sworn enemies of the people of Israel. When the Israelites got ready to enter the Promised Land, God told them to utterly wipe out the Canaanites—destroy their cities, kill their animals, and kill all the people—men and women, adults and children. Their religion was so toxic it was like spiritual Anthrax—so deadly it must be wiped out or the Israelites themselves would be infected.

Here is the line: Ham, Canaan, Canaanites, idolatry, immorality, enemies of God's people. This is historically how things developed over the centuries. When viewed from this perspective, Noah's words make perfect sense. Noah saw in Ham's act of disrespect a cavalier attitude toward sexual morality that was shared by his son Canaan. That seed would produce a vast harvest of evil in the Canaanites. Let them be slaves! This is God's judgement on their sin.

That leads to an important point. There is such a thing as Spiritual DNA. Just as your physical traits are passed down to your children, even so your personal strengths and weaknesses are passed down as well. Years ago I remember hearing a father warn his children that he had a temper and that they were likely to have a problem with anger as well. Many parents wouldn't do that, but perhaps we could help our children if we were more honest about our sins so that our children could be forewarned. Under the leading of the Holy Spirit, Noah looked into the future and saw that Ham's evil deed was symptomatic of a deeper rebellion against God, against the family, against decency, and against morality. He knew that tendency would only get worse and so he pronounced a prophetic curse on Canaan and the Canaanites.

Did this curse literally come true? Yes. The Canaanites were eventually wiped out. Though it took almost 1,500 years after the Jews entered the Promised Land, the Canaanites eventually disappeared from the face of the earth.

The fundamental issue of race and racism.

What does this curse have to do with the other descendants of Ham? Answer: Nothing at all. The curse was only upon Canaan, not upon the other three sons of Ham. Furthermore, this curse has nothing to do with skin colour. It has nothing to do with whether or not your ancestors came from Africa. It has nothing to do with what "race" of people you come from. It has nothing to do with whether or not you are black or white or any other colour or shade or hue. The Canaanites weren't black. They were closer to being white than black.

What does this story have to do with supporting slavery? Nothing at all, except that misguided people used this text to justify an evil system.

What does it have to do with supporting racial segregation? Again, nothing at all, except that misguided people used this text to justify an evil system. This passage is fascinating and historically interesting but it has nothing to do with race relations in the 21st century. Noah pronounced the curse on the Canaanites, and that curse was historically fulfilled before Christ was born. How do I know that? Look around. We've got all kinds of people living in most communities, some of them pretty unusual, but I don't see any Canaanites. They've been gone for over 2,000 years.

Does this passage have any contemporary applications? Absolutely! Here are a few of them. Honour your parents. Uphold the family. Don't gossip about the weakness of others. Remember that love covers a multitude of sins. Beware of the dangers of alcohol. Cover yourself up. Remember that modesty is a godly virtue. Especially this - take God and his Word seriously. Play by the rules and you'll be blessed and your family will be blessed. If you break the rules, especially the rules about the family and sexual purity, you and your family will pay a heavy price, sometimes for many years to come.

As the Lord himself said, "Those who honour me, I will honour." Those who dishonour God will be judged by him. In light of how this passage has been so badly misused, let us resolve to be the family of God together.
Love one another.
Accept one another.
Bear with one another.
Forgive one another.
Encourage one another.
Bear one another's burdens.
Honour one another.
Live in peace with one another.
Pray for one another.

"Make every effort to keep the unity of the Spirit through the bond of peace." "There is neither Jew nor Greek, slave nor free, male nor female, for you are all one in Christ Jesus."

We have different cultures, talents, gifts, and often we have different dreams. The things that unite us are far greater than the things that divide us. We are all made in God's image. All of us are sinners, no difference there. And all of us are saved by the same grace, all are redeemed by the blood of Christ, and all are indwelt by the same Holy Spirit. We worship the same God, read the same Bible, and we are all children of God through faith in Jesus Christ. If we stand, we stand by grace. If we live, we live by grace. When we all die, we will die by grace. We are all heirs of the same divine promises and partakers of the same divine nature. We have the same high priest in heaven who intercedes for us at the throne of grace. We are all given the same marching orders — Go into all the world and preach the gospel to every creature. And we have the same promise that nothing in all creation can separate us from the love of God in Christ Jesus.

Though we look different and act different, and sometimes we struggle to get along, and we don't always see eye to eye, we're all in this together. Someday when our earthly journey has come to an end, by God's grace we will all end up in the same place—together, forever, around the throne of God, in that vast multitude with the saints of all the ages, from every tribe and tongue and from every nation on earth, the Church Triumphant, singing, "Worthy is the Lamb that was slain." And so shall we ever be with the Lord. This is our hope, this is our destiny. Not just for some of us but for all who believe in Jesus. The things that unite us are far greater than the things that divide us. Though we have our preferences, and though we live in a world that likes to divide people by skin colour and language and age and money and nationality, still we gladly proclaim that by God's Grace, in Jesus Christ we will not be divided; we will stand together, side by side, shoulder to shoulder, united in Christ, now and forever.

At first glance Genesis 10 would not seem to offer much. The last verse of Genesis 10 summarises the chapter: "These are the clans of Noah's sons, according to their lines of descent, within their nations. From these the nations spread out over the earth after the flood". Perhaps an illustration will help. If you have ever played the board game Risk, you know that it contains a large map of the world. The object of the game is simple: Defeat all the other players and end up ruling the world. Each player is given armies of a different colour—blue or red or black or brown or yellow or green. The first step in the game is for the players to put their armies one by one on various countries or regions on the board—Great Britain, Greenland, Japan, India, the Middle East, the Congo, Western United States, and so on. When all the armies are in place, the game can begin. But there is a moment—it happens in every game—just before the first player takes his turn, when everyone stops and studies the board to see the alignment of forces. "He's really strong in Africa." "I'll bet he makes a move for Europe." "I'm going to fight him for South America." "If he gets India, he'll take all of Asia." And on it goes. There is a moment, always, when all the armies are in place and the fighting is about to begin, that things grow silent. Then someone rolls the dice and the armies go into battle.

Genesis 10 is like that moment just before the first player takes his turn. It's a snapshot of the ancient world showing how the nations are arrayed in and around the Middle East, especially around the Holy Land. This is what the world looks like just before the "game" begins. Those who have studied this chapter in detail remark on its amazing historical accuracy. It reveals the "genius of the Hebrew mind" and gives us a peek behind the curtain into the misty far reaches of early world history. There are 70 separate names here. Some of those names are people, some are names of cities, and others are names of tribes or nations or people groups.

This is *World History 101* as taught by Moses who was inspired by the Holy Spirit. If you enjoy history and geography and anthropology, and if you like to make connections between the ancient world and the 21st-century, then you'll enjoy Genesis 10. And all of us can gain something from this chapter because this is where we came from. This is our family tree! We are all in here somewhere. Commenting on this chapter, Martin Luther said, "Look into the historical accounts of all nations. If it were not for Moses alone, what would you know about the origin of man?" We would not know these things if God did not tell us.

Science and research alone can never tell us. Luther called this passage a "mirror" to see who we really are. We are so marred with sin, so divided from one another, that we cannot know our own history unless God himself tells us. This chapter is a sacred thread that joins the early morning of earth history to the rest of the Bible, and ultimately to you and to me.

It is easy to grow narrow and provincial and to say, "Us four and no more." Just my kind, colour, culture, language, people, background, tradition and preferences. Pretty soon you end up with a church all by yourself because no one else fits there. Christ came to redeem us from our smallness, our narrowness. Jesus said, "Go and teach all nations," and "My house shall be called a house of prayer for all nations."

The great Apostle Paul declared, "I am a debtor to all men." We are called to care for the people of the world. Christianity will not allow the heart to be small, but opens the heart to the whole wide world of men and women made in God's image. If we have narrow visions and small ideas and exclusive claims that we are better than others because of our heritage or background or skin colour, then we do not understand the gospel message.

Genesis 10 emphasises this truth by the very fact that the nations are listed by clans and languages, in their territories and nations. I have often meditated on the amazing words of Acts 17:26, "From one man he made every nation of men, that they should inhabit the whole earth; and he determined the times set for them and the exact places where they should live." The King James Version of the first phrase is very picturesque: God "hath made of one blood" all the nations that dwell on the earth. One blood. What a powerful image. There is only one blood - *human blood*. It flows in endless varieties but it is all "one blood."

The theory of racial superiority has led to horrible results in history. The Nazis elevated the "pure Aryan" race and used that as an excuse to murder 12 million Jews, Slavs, Ukrainians,

Russians, and others deemed inferior and unworthy. Against the evils of racism Paul declares, "We're all from the same stock. Fruit from the same branch. Born into the same human family." This is the basis for Christian reconciliation between the races and the various ethnic groups in society and in the church.

It is also confirmed by common sense. The more you travel around the world, the more common humanity seems to be. Superficially we are very different in our appearance, background, language and customs. But scratch deeper and you discover that all people are substantially the same. Once past the surface, you discover no fundamental difference between a man in the jungle and a corporate lawyer in the city. Everywhere we are the same—the same longings, regrets, dreams, hopes, the same need to love and be loved, the same desire to bear children and raise a family, with the same sense that there must be a God of some kind who made us.

As long as we live together on the earth there will be various races, colours, pigments, backgrounds, languages and cultures. These differences are not evil and should not be ignored or deprecated. There is much to appreciate in the various differences in humanity. But let us be clear on this point: There is only one race in God's eyes—the human race. Secondary differences do not matter to him the way they seem to matter so much to us. Paul's point is clear. Since we all descend from the same person, there is no room for inordinate pride or a feeling of superiority over others. We're all in this together—and we all need the saving touch of Jesus Christ. This truth provides the biblical basis for civil rights and for fair treatment of all people. This is the biblical argument against all prejudice and racial discrimination.

Ray Stedman called his sermon on Genesis 10, *"God's Funnel."* A funnel is an instrument for concentrating the flow of something from a wide area into a small area. That's what's happening here. Although it appears that God is working only with nations, the end of the chapter reminds us that the line of promise goes from one man to another. Shem is the neck of the funnel. The line that started with Adam goes to Noah, then to Shem, on to Peleg, eventually to Abraham, and thousands of years later will climax with the birth of Jesus Christ in Bethlehem. The flow of the biblical story moves from many nations to one man, Abraham, through whom all the nations on earth will be blessed. And how will this blessing come to the nations? Through the ultimate "Seed of Abraham," the Lord Jesus Christ.

Thus at the end of Genesis 10, we come face to face with Jesus Christ. He is the goal of every part of the Bible. Genesis 10 ends with the nations divided and in rebellion against God. And to a world in a rebellion, God says, "I love you! I love you! I love you!" This is the message of the gospel. And the question becomes very personal. If God has arranged all the events of history to bring his Son to the world, then you must eventually answer this question: "What have you done with Jesus?" Truth demands a personal response. All that I have said is just an academic exercise if it does not lead you to personal faith in Christ.

History is *His* Story.

You cannot live without him. He is the way, the truth and the life. No one comes to the Father except through Jesus.

In her book *God's Story*, Anne Graham Lotz tells the following story. Elizabeth Carter was a young American woman who taught English in mainland China. On a weekend outing with friends, she hiked up Tai Shan, a holy mountain, not too far from the city where she worked. At the base of the mountain, as she began her ascent, she saw an old beggar sitting by the path. She felt very impressed to speak with him and tell him about God. Because her friends hurried on up the path, Elizabeth suppressed the urge to stop and speak, and so she passed him by. During the afternoon exploration on the mountain, her thoughts kept returning to that old beggar. She began to deeply regret having not spoken to him, knowing that he would most likely have left before she returned. As she descended the summit in the early evening she resolved to make time to speak to him if he was still there. When Elizabeth reached the base of the mountain, to her eager surprise, the old beggar was still sitting exactly where he had been before. This time she went over to him and gently began to speak to him. She told him that there is a God Who created all things, that the great Creator God had created him because he loved him and wanted to be known by him. She told the old man that God had sent his Son to die on a cross as a sacrifice for the man's sin, and that if he placed his faith in God's Son, Jesus, he would be forgiven and would receive eternal life. As Elizabeth continued telling the old man about God, tears began to slip down his weather-beaten face, moistening his few wispy white whiskers. Thinking she had offended him in some way, Elizabeth asked what was wrong. The old man smiled through his tears and said softly, 'I have worshiped him all my life. I just didn't know his name.'

The specific circumstances of your life do not change the fundamental truth. All of us were with born a desire to know the God who made us. But most people living on earth do not really know his Name. His name is Jesus. Here is the question you must answer: "What have you done with Jesus?" History truly is His Story. You cannot live without him. What have you done with Jesus?

Chapter 6
The Work of Faith
Hebrews 11:7

Hebrews 11:7, "By *faith* Noah, when warned about things not yet seen, in holy fear built an ark to save his family. By his *faith* he condemned the world and became heir of the righteousness that comes by faith."

A special movie was on T.V. It boasted an all-star line up and a special effects budget of many millions. The movie was disappointing to say the least. I say this because they got the story of Noah all wrong. They portrayed Lot as his best friend when in scripture Lot never even knew Noah. They lived hundreds of years apart. They had the destruction of Sodom and Gomorrah occurring before the flood instead of afterwards as it is recorded in God's Word! The script of the movie even had God threatening to kill Noah after he had faithfully built the ark. It was a fiasco. Let's get the real story because according to the New Testament, Noah is listed in Hebrews 11 as a hero of the faith.

We've spent time in previous chapters in Genesis 9 and 10. Let us go back for just a moment more to get a good picture in our mind's eye of the setting of this historic event which is recorded.

Examine Noah himself.

His grandfather was Methuselah -- who still holds the record when it comes to the longest life span....remember he lived 969 years! Noah's name means "comfort" or "rest." Scripture says that his father, Lamech, gave him this name because, as a baby, Noah, comforted him as he laboured to work the ground that had been cursed due to the sin of Adam and Eve. And Noah himself was a father. He had three sons, named Shem, Ham, and Japheth. Scripture also says that Noah was a righteous man.

Righteous man

In Genesis 6:9 it says, "Noah was a righteous man, blameless among the people of his time." The word "blameless" doesn't mean perfection. It literally means uncontaminated." As we shall see, Noah was not "contaminated" by the wickedness of his day. He was Gods' man through and through. Clarence MacCartney calls Noah, "the solitary Saint." For, Noah, was the only one of his kind, which tells us that solitary goodness is possible. Noah lived in a culture that was unimaginably degraded, horribly corrupt and yet he was different. He was the only man of faith in an entire world that had turned it's back on God.

Henry David Thoreau once said, "If I seem to walk out of step with others, it is because I am listening to another drum beat." And this is a good description of genuine faith. Christians who embrace a deep faith in God walk through life as though listening to another drum beat. They are out of step with the world. You see, there is no such thing as a Christian life that is not counter-culture. If you are a follower of the Lord, it means you are going to have to make decisions that distinguish you from the sinful world in which we all live.

Paul said that if we live out our faith, "we will shine as stars in the universe, amidst a crooked and depraved generation." No one can thoroughly participate in everything that's true of our culture today and follow Christ at the same time. This is tough. We follow a narrow path! It's difficult to be a young adult in university or wherever and stand alone for God. It's difficult, but Noah's life proves that it is possible! God needs individuals who are willing to stand alone for Him if need be.

Walked with God

Then Genesis 6:9 says something else about Noah. He walked with God. Enoch also walked with God. In fact in all history, Noah and Enoch are the only two men of whom this is said. Walking with God means to move in the same direction in which God is going. It means keeping in step with God. Noah and Enoch didn't run ahead of God, nor did they lag behind. They kept step with God. Think about it. When you're walking with someone, you're not moving so fast that conversation is difficult. You can enjoy your companion. And this sharing makes everything else enjoyable. You can look together at the cloud formations, the turning of the leaves in the autumn, the flower beds in neighbour's gardens, or whatever.

Walking with someone is a great picture of intimacy. This kind of intimacy with God was a lifestyle for Noah. Year after year, for longer and longer periods of time during the day, he shared more and more of his life with God.

A man of obedience

Twice scripture speaks of his obedience. In Genesis 6:22, it says, "Noah did *everything,* just as God *commanded* him." In Genesis 7:5 we are told "Noah did *all* (not most, but all) that the Lord commanded him." Unlike many disciples today who pick and choose which commands of God they will apply to their lives, Noah embraced the kind of love for God that Jesus described when He said, "If you love Me, you will *obey* what I command."

I hope you see in Noah characteristics that you should emulate: a righteous life unpolluted by the world, a man who cherished and nourished an intimate daily walk with God, and an individual who showed his love for God with a lifestyle of obedience to His commands!

Unprecedented wickedness

To really understand Noah we also need to look at the culture in which he lived. Scripture teaches that it was a culture of unprecedented wickedness. Genesis 6:11 says, "Now the earth was corrupt in God's sight and was full of *violence*." Throughout the text the combination of the words "corrupt" and "violence" is repeated again and again and this is because the moral degradation of life, the corruption of ethics is always accompanied by violence, a warning that we should heed even in our day and age.

David Wilkerson has a fascinating and challenging insight on this. In a sermon he preached he ask, "When you hear the word "violence," what comes to mind? You probably think of the incredible things you hear on the radio or see in the newspapers." He goes on to say, "Our senses have become so overloaded with such images, we now try to shut them all out. We hate to even pick up a newspaper anymore! What forms of violence were there in Noah's day, that so riled the anger of God he finally cried "Enough!"? Did everyone carry a sword? Was it like Sodom, where roving gangs were ready to rape strangers? Was it a time of wars and ethnic tensions? There may have been some of these forms of violence. But there had to be others besides murder, bloodshed and perversion. You see, Scripture says that in these same violent days, the people "...were eating and drinking, marrying and giving in marriage, until the day that Noah entered into the ark." It was safe to go into the streets. People were buying and selling in the markets. Couples were getting engaged and having weddings. They were building houses, raising families. There isn't any mention of bloodshed. Yet the Bible says these were violent people!"

David Wilkerson writes, "Contrast that scene with our present day. Can you imagine what would have happened if Noah had tried to build the ark in some abandoned area in New York City? Do you know how long that work would have lasted? Within an hour there would have been camel races down 42nd Street! The wire fences protecting the ark would've been cut.

Noah's tools would have been stolen. Teenage gangs would have drilled holes in the ark's hull. The expensive gopher wood would've been taken apart by sections and hauled off. Pickup trucks would have been backing in and out all night long. And by daybreak all those exotic animals would have been hidden in apartments across the city!"

Think about it: In Noah's day, there was no sign of robbers, thieves or pranksters trying to burn down the ark. No one plundered his livestock or stole his hay. No one painted graffiti on the sides of the ark. Instead, Scripture says, for 120 years he walked to and fro, safely collecting his animals. He could eat, preach and go to weddings and never be in any danger.

There was something else going on in Noah's day. This society was so orderly, people could go on with their ordinary lives without any trouble. There had to be a different form of violence -- a kind engaged in by ordinary people who went about their daily affairs!

The form of violence in Noah's day that enraged God was mental violence!

"And God saw that the wickedness of man was great in the earth, and that every imagination of the thoughts of his heart was only evil continually." There it is - *mental violence!* Every imagination of the people's minds was corrupted! As any drug addict can tell you, the habit is in the mind. And there was something going on in the minds of the whole corrupted society of Noah's day! The Hebrew word for "violence" means "vicious dealings, mistreatment, wrongful imaginings, cruelty." All the bloodshed, murders, rapes, etc. that took place in that day were the fruit of a root of violence in the people's hearts and minds! The whole society -- every man, woman and accountable person - was gripped by mental forms of violence!

In the framework of God's definition of violence - the kind that possesses and rules the heart – people who read this could be violent people! That's right - many Christians are guilty of the kind of violence for which God destroyed the world! You may answer, "But I've never hurt anybody! I've never even entertained a thought of harming anyone. I'm a gentle, peace-loving person. I may have problems, but violence isn't one of them!" That all may be true of you. But you still may be a mentally violent person!

There is the mental violence of "bearing a grudge"! A grudge is any envy or ill-will toward another. There is a form of violence the Bible calls "enticement"! Encouraging people toward the wrong. However, the very worst kind of violence - the kind that offends God most deeply is found in Matthew 18:6, "Whoever causes one of these little ones who believe in Me to stumble, it is better for him that a heavy millstone be hung around his neck, and that he be drowned in the depth of the sea." You have heard that the Mafia rubs out an enemy by tying bundles of concrete to his feet and throwing him into a river. Jesus is saying this is exactly what is deserved by those who rob children of their faith in Christ!

What did Jesus see taking place in Noah's day? He saw hundreds of innocent children who loved the bearded old preacher! They loved playing with his animals -- and they loved what he preached. These kids must have asked their parents why no one obeyed what Noah said. But their parents mocked Noah! They said, "Don't go near that old man again!" Their parents chipped away at their faith with ridicule, shame, snide remarks. Too often, a child's worst danger of violence is in the home -- perpetrated by his own parents! There is a tidal wave of incest, child abuse, broken homes. Children are being neglected, abandoned, wounded, emasculated. God is concerned with an even more insidious form of violence toward children. The real violence -- the real stumbling block -- is a father who has neglected the call of God! He swears, curses, takes God's name in vain. He mistreats his wife, drinks -- and leads a devil's example for his children! This is not only abuse of his children -- it is violence against them! You may say, "I don't hit women! I've never lifted my hand against my kids. I'm not violent!" But your total neglect of God -- your neglect of His church, your lack of spiritual help to your family -- constitutes vicious violence! I see mothers who sit around smoking, drinking, telling dirty stories -- and then try to lecture their teenage kids about drugs! Mothers ought to raise their children in the fear and love of God.

Genesis 6:5 says that God saw this as a great wickedness. And it is tragic to note that prior to this chapter in Genesis, any time God gazed upon His creation, any time the phrase, *"God saw"* is used, it is followed by God commenting, "It was good." or "It was very good." Now God looks at the world and it is not good at all. It is totally corrupt. So much had changed! The human race was degraded almost beyond recognition. God was thoroughly disgusted with what He saw in the human race. Then, listen to the last part of verse 5, "every inclination of the thoughts of the hearts of men were evil all the time."

Corruption had become so thorough that there was nothing human left about these people. Even their thoughts were a constant mental stream of evil. They had already drowned everything "human" about themselves in a kind of moral wretchedness that had existed even before the rains began to fall. They had already destroyed themselves. So, the deluge was the logical outcome of the way of life these people had chosen.

Verse 6 is also significant in that it records not the anger of God but His grief over the fallen state of humanity. It says, "The Lord was grieved that He had made man on the earth, and His heart was filled with pain." God's heart ached as if He had lost something extraordinarily precious to Him. Then, we read of God's sorrowful determination to destroy not only human life but all other life as well. Every living creature was going to die in the flood except for the few animals that would be protected in the ark. That might seem excessive until we remember that human beings were made regents of earth, to have dominion over all created things and human corruption had apparently spread so that it ruined almost everything else. It's like we see today when scientists make mistakes and spread radioactive waste over a large area so that everything that comes in contact with it is contaminated and will pose a threat for thousands of years polluting air and water and all life. Something like that evidently had happened in the days before the flood. Human fools had ruined life everywhere and there was very little left that was worth saving.

That is the story. Let us see what it can teach about *faith.* I want to point our three things that Noah, this hero of the faith, has taught us when it comes to this subject:

Noah's life shows us that true faith has a BASIS.

It has something to back it up. Noah would say that faith in God is not a hunch. It's not positive thinking. It's not a leap in the dark. Noah would tell us that faith has a basis, a foundation. Hebrews 11:7 says Noah did what he did, "...when warned by God...about things not yet seen." The word "warned" means Noah was divinely instructed. God spoke to him and told him what He was going to do. So the *basis* of Noah's faithful actions was the Word of God.

The Bible teaches this principle of faith. In Romans 10 it says, that, "faith comes by hearing and hearing by the Word of God." Genuine faith has a basis. It is founded on the things God says. In fact a faith that doesn't rest on the Word of God is not a faith worth having. True faith has a sure foundation. It is not based on our feelings or emotions. It is not based on our traditions. Our source of authority, the basis of our faith, is the Word of God!

Note that the text says that God warned Noah of a thing, *"not yet seen."* God's Word that the flood was to come was all that Noah had to go on. There was no visible sign of an impending flood. It was 120 years out there in the future. And what is worse. Noah had never seen rain. The Bible infers that it had never rained until the flood came. Genesis 2 says that, "God had not sent rain on the earth but streams came up from the earth and watered the whole surface of the ground." Noah had never seen a flood, for you can't have a flood unless you have rain. I am sure that Noah's peers laughed at him as he built a boat 500 miles from the nearest ocean and a thousand times too big for his family and then began to fill it with the animals that God sent. Noah had nothing to base his actions on other than God's Word. I doubt if you or I would have trusted God under these circumstances, but Noah had the faith to do so. He believed God's Word. Noah accepted what God told him. For 120 years he worked on this huge ark on the basis of God's Word alone! And in all that time, nothing happened to make him think it was going to come true.

It might have been easier for Noah if every three or four days God had blown up some clouds and let some lightening flash and thunder roll. That might have been encouraging to Noah. This didn't happen! If Noah could believe and obey God's Word for 120 years under those conditions, then surely you and I ought to be able to do so with the fuller revelation that we have. We have an entire Bible filled with God's Words upon which to base our faith. We have His risen Son to guide us through life. We know that God's words are true!

Do you hear the words to a famous hymn ringing in your heads?
"How firm a foundation ye saints of the Lord
is fixed for your faith in His excellent WORD!
What more can He say than to you He has said?
To you who for refuge to Jesus have fled?"

Our faith does have a firm foundation. For, a person who embraces this kind of faith build's their life on the Word of God. Just as God promised in the days of Noah to destroy the world because of man's wickedness, so He has promised that He will destroy the world again! In 2 Peter God cites the example of Noah and the flood and then in chapter 3 verse 10 it says, "But the day of the Lord will come like a thief. The heavens will disappear with a roar; the elements will be destroyed by fire, and the earth and everything in it will be destroyed." This text goes on to ask us, in light of this, based on this Word of God, what kind of persons ought we to be? What kind of lives should we live? Well it doesn't say we should build an ark but verse 14 does command that we make every effort to live lives that are "spotless and blameless."

Noah's life shows us that our faith in God has a basis. Our faith is founded on God's word. The things He has said.

If someone lives by faith it will be EVIDENT in their life.

Faith is not an invisible thing. It shows! Hebrews 11:7 says that Noah *did something* because of his faith! He built a huge ark, something everyone noticed! Noah's faith expressed itself in obedience to God's commands. Real faith, genuine faith, always expresses itself in that way. Faith always acts!

These days, there is a common misconception that thinks of men and women of faith as so occupied with the future that they sit around twiddling their thumbs doing nothing in the now. It has been said that people like this are so "heavenly minded that they are no earthly good." But living this way is not faith! It is fatalism! Faith works! Faith does something now in view of the future! So if we fold our hands and wait for the second coming we are not living a life of faith. Faith is not passive, it is dynamic and forceful.

Read this magnificent summary of the actions of faith in Hebrews 11:32, "And what more shall I say? For time would fail me to tell you of Gideon, Barak, Samson, Jephthah, of David and Samuel and the prophets - who, *through faith,* conquered kingdoms, enforced justice, received promises, stopped the mouths of lions, quenched raging fire, escaped the edge of the sword, won strength out of weakness, became mighty in war, put foreign armies to flight." Note, these words are not poetry. They are history! This is faith at work. These activities of faith have changed the course of history.

Noah did something about his faith. He built an ark. Noah didn't just call *Home Delivery* and tell them to deliver the lumber for the ark! No, Noah and Shem and Ham and Japheth had to cut all those trees and saw them into lumber. This was way before the advent of power tools! In other words, it was a big job! No wonder it took them well over a century to complete it. You can understand how Noah must have been considered the biggest fool in all of history. People saw that great hulk of a boat being built and they must have laughed themselves silly.

We have not been told to build an ark. That was done once and for all. God will never flood the earth again. Every time you see a rainbow remind yourself of that truth! But Christ is the "ark of salvation." 1 Peter 3:20 teaches that the flood story is a picture of the coming of Christ. So let's pause to note the parallels.

There is no way in our own strength to escape the problem of our sinfulness. We need a Saviour just like Noah needed that ark. We need Jesus. We need some body to gather us in and protect us.

Another parallel is this. Just as the flood came suddenly, another cataclysm is coming. People in Noah's day were eating and drinking and going to weddings and living out their corrupt, but comfortable, existence when the deluge abruptly came. And some day Christ will come suddenly.

Just like Noah there is a lot of work for us to do. As Christians, we are called to "people" the ark. Jesus said, "You shall be witnesses unto Me." Our work of faith is to share the good news that people may be saved by entering the ark of safety provided by Christ. To do this we must have the faith of Noah. A faith that expresses itself in works. Because as James writes, "faith without works is dead."

I read a story once about an old fisherman who kept two oars in his boat, and on one he had written the word, "FAITH" and on the other, the word, "WORKS." Someone asked him why He did that. And he said, "Well, get in the boat and I'll show you."

So they boarded and went out into the river and the fisherman picked up the oar that said "FAITH" and started paddling with it on one side. And the boat started going around and around in circles and drifting with the current of the river. So he looked at the one who had asked the question and said, "That doesn't work does it?" Then he put down the "FAITH" oar and took up the oar with the word, "WORKS" on it and he put it in the other side and started paddling. And again the boat started going around in circles...spinning the other way this time as it drifted with the current. So he said, "That doesn't work either, does it?" Well, then he took both oars and started paddling on both sides of the boat and the boat made progress in the right direction. It moved against the current of the river. The obvious point of this story is that you need both FAITH and WORKS to get anywhere in the Christian life. FAITH without works doesn't amount to much. If we have faith but not works then as Paul wrote to the Ephesians, we will be "...tossed back and forth ....around and around in circles... by the waves, and blown here and there by every wind of teaching and by the cunning and craftiness of men in their deceitful scheming."

A look at Noah's life shows us that faith has a *basis*. It is founded on the Word of God. His life also shows that genuine faith has a visible expression. Faith and *works* literally go hand in hand. We can learn one more thing about faith from Noah's life..

Stronger faith.

We see that storms like Noah endured stretches and matures our faith in God. They develops us into stronger, more fully-developed disciples. This truth is seen when we look at the way Noah's voyage of faith ended. Scripture says that after 150 days, the rains finally stopped. And at this point there is a very stark statement in scripture.

Look at Genesis 7:23, "Every living thing on the face of the earth was wiped out; men and animals and the creatures that move along the ground and the birds of the air were wiped from the earth." Notice the next phrase, *"Only Noah was left..."* Imagine how Noah felt as the wind and the rain stopped and the waves disappeared and the boat stopped moving and floated in calm waters. Everything was gone. Death was everywhere. And there was only silence and darkness. Remember, the boat was closed in everywhere. Perhaps it was more like a huge coffin than anything else we can imagine covered with pitch inside and out.

Genesis 6:16 has an ambiguous phrase that is probably describing a small window. It was covered over during the storm. And the door through which the animals and people entered was closed by God and covered over with pitch. So, Noah couldn't see out or if he could it was only through the window near the top so he could look only upward not downward. This helps us see why it was hard for Noah to see if the waters were receding. He couldn't look down and see if the ground was dry. Another thing I want you to notice is that Noah was told very little about what would happen to him in the end when he began this adventure. He had obeyed God's verbal instructions but now God was silent. As Noah floated on the water all these months, encased in this great wooden structure, there was no explanation, no prompting, no voice of hope from God.

In Genesis 6:18 God had spoken to Noah and said he was the only righteous one in all his generation, the only one who had a heart for God. God had given him His word by saying, "I will establish my covenant with you and you will enter the ark-you and your sons and your wife and your sons' wives with you." But Noah didn't hear any thing about getting out of the ark, about the end of the story. And now Noah goes through 150 days of floating with no word from God, encased in a place where he couldn't see out or get information. I imagine that every hour of every day he wondered when and how it was all going to end, but he had no word from God as to what the end of the story would be.

Noah waited and waited. Have you ever had a time like that? When God seemed to be silent? After floating silently for five months without being able to see where he was going, having no idea of the conditions outside the boat, wondering if it would ever come to an end, things finally began to happen. The Bible says, "God remembered Noah." He sent a wind to move the ark and the waters receded and the ark came to rest in the mountains of Ararat. You can imagine Noah's relief to know that the ark was not going to be his home forever. The first thing Noah did was to remove the covering and saw that the ground was dry. This was ten and a half months after the flood began. He saw that the water had receded but Noah didn't come out yet. Then a month and 27 days later he could see that it was growing increasingly dry. But Noah still did not come out of the ark, not until God finally spoke again and invited him out.

What effect did this time of God's silence have on Noah? Let's do a little "before and after" comparing to answer this question. Before the flood Noah was the only righteous person on the earth. 2 Peter 2:5 says he was "...*the* preacher of righteousness." With all the corrupted half-demon people running around, he must have felt that he was pretty special. But when he floated in the boat, when he seemed forgotten by God, he was able to notice the tension that existed between him and his sons and their families. He understood his capacity to be angry with God, and to feel sorry for himself. The awful realisation dawned on Noah that he was going to start the world again, and his heart was as much in need of the grace of God as anyone else. He saw that he was not a good specimen on which to build a new earth. He found out that he was as capable of tawdry and angry and embarrassing and godless behaviour as anyone else. This time of silence showed Noah all this. Doesn't God often teach us lessons like this when He's quiet?

As long as we can compare ourselves to other people, we can fool ourselves. But when we are put in some kind of wilderness

92

and there's nothing but the spiritual reality of who we are on the inside to occupy our thoughts, the awful discovery begins to take place: We see that we are capable of sin. We see that we are not as great and courageous and godly as we think we are. We discover our weakness and shortcomings.

When the day finally came to break the seal, open the door, and see the world, Noah was a man who had discovered his own inadequacy. He would not come out until God invited him out. I imagine he wanted nothing more than to set his feet on solid ground but he didn't. He didn't step out and leap into the arms of his Lord, because his own failures were still ringing in his mind. In fact, the first thing he did when he came out was to build an altar and offer a sacrifice to God. This was the first altar of worship to God that is mentioned in scripture. And I think it was both a sin offering and a thank offering. It was a way for Noah to both thank God for His protection and to say, "I need you God. Please save me from the sins I've discovered in my heart."

God used this time of silence to change Noah, to mature his faith and make him into a man who realised how much he needed God. The type of person on whom God could rebuild humanity. That is how it is with us. In fact, the kind of faith that God values most develops in these times when He seems to be silent.

Paul Tournier said, "Where there is no longer any opportunity for doubt, there is no longer any opportunity for faith." And he was right, for faith, real faith, demands uncertainty and confusion. It requires times of silence from God to test it and make it stronger. Years ago I fractured my shoulder when I was knocked off my bike by a car when cycling. The doctor told me it would be less likely to break in the same spot than any where else because it was stronger there now than it was before. The stress of the fracture and the subsequent mending of the bone made it stronger at the point of the break.

The stress of silence can make our faith in God stronger.

Philip Yancey teaches that there are basically two kinds of faith....the childlike trust that God can do anything...which is the kind of faith that young David had when he went toe-to-toe with Goliath. And then there is that "hang-on-to-God-no-matter-what" kind of faith....which is what Job and the heroes of the faith in Hebrews 11 practised. As Christians we need both. For childlike trust may not survive times in an ark when God seems to be silent...times when we are overcome with the evil in the world around us. Such times call for something more...a deeper, stronger faith. This kind of faith is embraced by mature disciples who have learned that even when we cannot see God at work or hear His voice, even then we believe that He still reigns and has not abandoned us. This is the kind of faith that Noah developed in that ark. It is the kind of faith Job had when in the midst of his troubles he exclaimed, "Though He slay me....yet will I trust Him."

Yancey writes, "Paradoxically, the most perplexing, Job-like times may help 'fertilise faith and nurture intimacy with God. The deepest faith...sprouts at a point of contradiction, like a blade of grass between stones. Human beings grow by striving, working, stretching."

Only the storms of life can grow our faith to this level of maturity. So let's review what the real story of Noah has taught us about faith. Genuine faith is not wishful thinking, it has a solid *basis,* it is founded on the *Word of God.* Real faith *works!* It acts! People *see* our faith by the way that we live. Finally, Noah's experience shows us that our faith is *strengthened* and matured in times of crisis when God seems to be silent.

Noah didn't save millions or even thousands. But he saved his family. I regard this as a remarkable accomplishment.

How did Noah save his family?

First, by example. Noah was a just man in his generation. And Noah walked with God. Secondly, by teaching them. He was called a preacher of righteousness. He warned all men of the approaching flood but succeeded only with his family. I regard that as successful preaching.

Think for a moment. Why will you thank God? Will it be because this was the day you decided to put your faith in His Word accepting His forgiveness through His Son, entering the ark of salvation that is found only in Jesus Christ? Or, will you thank God for using today to help you see your need to live out your faith in such a way that your people see your faith just as they saw Noah's when he built that boat? It may be that you are thanking God for our Bible because it helped you better understand a time when He has been silent. Perhaps God has helped you to see some trial you are enduring...some storm that is raging in your life as something that has actually strengthened your faith.